FUCK THEM! YOU TRIED, MOVE ON!

The modern breakup

E. ARAS

CONTENTS

INTRODUCTION

If you are reading this book, it is because you feel you're identifying or resonating with it. Maybe you recently had a nasty breakup or you've not been able to keep a relationship and you are beginning to think something is wrong with you. It is not you and it is not me: there are millions of women who are trying to understand male behavior. We spend a lot of time thinking about all our failed relationships, asking why things didn't work with that man that you liked so much. Then there's all that time you've spent thinking about what you might have done wrong on a date and why he hasn't reached out to you yet. There are innumerable questions that arise in our minds about romantic relationships.

For a long time, I thought I had a problem. I observed many "happy" couples and I felt bad that I was not part of one of them. If you wonder why the "happy" is in quotes, it's because who knows if they are really happy? To take that idea even further, who says that happiness depends on being in a relationship? Being in a relationship is not an obligation, and we must learn and be clear about that. There is nothing wrong with us as women because we haven't had a successful relationship: there's nothing wrong with you, or with me, or my friend, or my cousin, or the millions of women around the world reading this.

You are in the wrong place, darling, if you are reading this thinking I will give you the key to finding your Prince Charming and living happily ever after. I want you to read this to understand that you are valuable, that you do not need anyone, that you must have independence in all aspects of your life including emotional independence, and whoever you end up dating should feel lucky to be in your life. I especially want to tell you that your life doesn't have to revolve around a man. A man should bring extra spice to your life to make it better; he should not add problems or make you feel underrated.

I'm clarifying that this book is not about lying to you to console you or tell you what you think you want to hear. I am not going to tell you how to get your ex back or how to get a man. I am going to be realistic because I learn from my mistakes and I am writing this book to share these lessons in the hope that others can benefit from my experience. We are going to learn how to be in control of our lives as women and how to defy societal stereotypes and find happiness.

I hope that the information in this book will be useful to you, and that you will have fun while identifying with the topics. I also hope you will keep an open mind while reading this book, because without an open mind, the information in this book won't achieve its aim. If you really want to be in control of your life as a single lady and build the kind of life you've always wanted, despite that nasty break up, then go ahead and keep an open mind.

CHAPTER ONE: BREAK UP - CRY YOUR TEARS

Breakups hurt, and <u>pain demands to be felt.</u> So, feel the pain and cry your tears. You thought things were going well, and he suddenly upped and left. Or he chose someone else over you and you can't understand how he could choose her over you because she doesn't even measure up to your standards. Maybe you still love someone who no longer loves you, or never loved you and never will.

Maybe your ex changed in unbelievable ways and you had to leave because the relationship had become unhealthy and toxic. Another scenario is that he decided being alone was better than being in a relationship with you and you can't understand why he chose nothing over you.

Whether you decided to break up with him or he decided to break up with you or the break up was a mutual decision, it is bound to hurt. It can leave you feeling like you weren't enough, or there was something you could have done better or maybe if you had tried harder, it might have worked out. A breakup can deal a serious blow to your self-esteem.

Take a minute to breathe because all of these thoughts can be totally overwhelming. Stop thinking about what you could have done differently. Stop thinking the breakup was your fault. Don't even blame him. Stop all of that!

<u>You shouldn't have to fight for someone to love you</u>. You deserve to be loved in a healthy and beautiful way. You shouldn't have to change into someone else for someone to love you; you are amazing the way you are. You shouldn't have to compete with other ladies for a guy's attention; you are unique. I'm going to tell you this and I need you to believe me: you are enough and worthy of love without having to beg or fight for it.

While a breakup can be heart wrenching, it is actually the best time to do an evaluation and make positive changes. I understand the fact that you need to feel the pain and accept what happened, maybe even cry a couple of times, but at some point, you have to get over it. There are three options to choose from: you can choose to wallow in self-pity, hate and resentment trying to get your ex back and not get over the breakup; you can decide to move on as if it never even happened and end up repeating the same mistakes over and over again; or you can decide to take time after a breakup to heal properly, re-evaluate and take back control of your life. The third option is guaranteed to lead to long term happiness and a more fulfilling and fruitful relationship when you eventually decide to start one.

Most times, people pick the first option because it is the easiest and then spend a lot of time on it. When it eventually doesn't work out, they move on to the next option. Then they keep repeating the same cycle of heartbreak. Even though the prospect of the third option seems inviting, most people do not know how to go about it. That is what we are going to be learning in this book. But first, you must learn how to handle grief and work through it.

How do you navigate the path from loss and pain to healing and happiness?

You navigate the path by putting yourself first before anything else, developing yourself while allowing yourself to feel all the emotions that keep popping up. It is very important to not suppress any emotion. While taking care of yourself, it's okay to break down and feel all of these emotions, as long as you don't stay there. You have to pick yourself up and continue your journey to healing.

By default, in nature, when something leaves your life, it has to be replaced with something else. This is why a lot of people end one relationship and immediately jump into another. This is why rebound relationships happen. When you get rid of a toxic partner or leave a relationship, you will be tempted to replace your ex with someone else. Don't do this. If you immediately get into another relationship, it's bound to be a mirror of your previous relationship. You will make the same mistakes, and end up being heartbroken again. So, what do you do? Find something else to fill the vacuum. Not someone else, something else. Pick up a new hobby, a new goal, learn something new. Find something to fill up the space and the time that would've been spent with him. When you are gainfully occupied, you won't have the time to think about getting him back or even to miss him. Plus, you'll also learn a skill that might come in handy in the future. It's a win-win.

As well as replacing him with something else in your life, you also have to replace your negative emotions with positive emotions. You have to be intentional about this process. You not only want to get rid of the negative emotions, you also want to be sure you are replacing them with positive ones. Drop the hate and replace it with self-love. Drop the bitterness and replace it with a good self-image. Drop the resentment and replace it with forgiveness.

Make sure he doesn't rent a space in your head. Instead of being emotionally invested in hating or resenting him, you need to be invested in loving yourself and seeing how amazing you are. Whenever the thought pops up that you weren't good enough for him, replace it with a word of affirmation that you are enough. Whenever you feel like you are not worthy of love, tell yourself that you deserve to be loved without begging for it. Whenever you're tempted to compare yourself to his present girlfriend, tell yourself that you are unique and that comparing yourself to another person is an insult. You need to let the past lose its hold over you.

After you've learned how to take away whatever hold the past has over you, you can then proceed to building yourself up. I know that right now you are an amazing lady, but there's always room for improvement. You need to make sure that you are not stuck in a place after the breakup. I know it's easy to feel lost after a breakup, especially when you were with him for a very long time. You can begin to feel like you no longer know who you are when he's no longer in the picture. That's because a major part of your life revolved around him and you no longer know who you are. It's very normal to feel this way. It might even make you miss him more or want him back because you feel like you can't live without him. Drop the phone! You don't need him. Look, allow yourself to feel lost, confused, frustrated, and miss him if you have to. But you do not need him back.

After feeling all you want to feel, it is time to start building yourself back up. Set goals for yourself and write them down. Pick up new hobbies or learn a new skill. You need to do things that'll build you up as a person. In addition to this, you need to socialize. Go out, meet new people, or meet up with old friends. Getting out and socializing takes your mind off things and strengthens your relationships with your friends. You have to be careful, though, not to get involved with any of them. It's easy to get attached to someone else because you're both spending time together while you are emotionally vulnerable. Be careful to avoid this.

Starting now, put yourself first. You need to take care of yourself because you are going to need strength to face your feelings and to revisit the past. At this point, you are allowed to be a bit selfish. Put yourself first, take care of yourself without thinking about anybody else. Build your self-esteem by affirming yourself. Speak positively to yourself, think positive thoughts, do nice things for yourself, avoid self-destructive behaviours, focus on your goals, your hobbies, interests and don't forget to meet up with friends regularly.

You need to create a rhythm or routine that works for you. It is absolutely necessary to have things going on in your life. When you have a full and blissful life, you are careful of the people you let into your life. Being careful helps you make better choices because you know the effort you put in to getting to where you are.

The first rule of taking care of yourself is to not contact your ex. I know a lot of people believe they can still be friends with their ex after a breakup. As innocent and sincere as that is, you don't need to remain friends with him if you are going to heal properly. It is better to cut off contact with him.

In the world now, it is very easy to contact someone; it is therefore necessary to make the decision not to contact him or be available for him to contact you. With all the social media tools we have now, contacting him can be as easy as leaving a comment on his Instagram post or tagging him on another post. There are so many easy ways of contacting him: without a strong resolution to cut off all contact, you will end up reaching out. In addition, if he tries to contact you, you will need a strong resolution to not pick up the phone or not respond.

It is going to be very difficult to cut off all contact with him. I mean, you spent a lot of your time with him and a part of you still might want him back. But, truth be told, if you contact him, you will only be stalling your healing. It's in your best interest to not fall for the temptation to text him, call, leave a voicemail, comment on or like his posts. Trust me, this tough decision will pay off in the long run. It's not easy but it is what you need to do. If you have to delete his number and unfollow him on social media, then do what you have to do. You're not being petty, you're trying to get over him.

Keeping this commitment when you feel down and frustrated can seem daunting. There can be times when you miss him so much that you feel like you have to get in touch with him. This urge is expected, but learn to sit with it till it passes instead of picking up your phone to text or call him. Intellectually, you might realize you shouldn't be in touch, but then you think of a hundred different reasons you need to talk. Okay, set those reasons aside because they're not necessarily explanations: (they're excuses, and everyone has one or two favorites that stand in the way of their healing.) You need to know this: no excuse is good enough to reach out to your ex. Whenever you feel like picking up the phone to contact him, why don't you do something else instead? Take a shower, call a friend, watch a movie, work on a craft or hobby, go to the gym.

The key to getting better and moving on is to break completely away from the relationship and the person you've spent so much time with. As long as this person distracts you from your focus, it will be hard to put an end to the relationship and start a new chapter of your life. Continuing to contact or be available to be contacted only keeps you trapped, contributing to your hurt. It stops you from building a new life and keeps you aching for your old life. You seriously do not want that.

After you have cut ties with your ex, you need to know that any pain that isn't confronted doesn't go anywhere, it's inside and spreads like wildfire. If you deny that pain every time you end a relationship, you'll end up with a pile of unresolved sorrow, making each loss increasingly more difficult to handle. When people are scared of being hurt, it's often because they haven't dealt with their loss and grief. The result is that their life becomes stiffer, their fear increases, and choices become harder to make. With unresolved sadness running the scene, it's hard to get close to people and trust anybody. Fear inspires a fight-or-flight response in us all.

When it comes to relationships, each person's flight response manifests differently. Some have trouble with intimacy. Some try to get close, feel stifled, then run away. Others react badly to fear with the fight response where they disintegrate into endless arguments or patterns of breakups and makeups after the initial "honeymoon" period is over. Most dysfunctional behavior in relationships is directly attributable to unaddressed loss in one or both partners. Resolving the loss ensures you won't be afraid anymore, allowing you to have happier and healthier relationships.

It might be convenient to avoid remembering the sadness while working through the disappointment following a breakup. At first, the process seems really daunting, because you have to confront your true feelings straight on. It may even seem easier to totally disregard your disappointment, but when you ignore loss, grief or pain, the mental strain exacts a very heavy price on you. By contrast, all positive things flow from healing unresolved loss. You may have had a lot of unresolved pain that may have resulted from a number of complicated relationships. Now you have the power to redefine the pattern, heal whatever you need to heal, and learn the lessons you need to learn. Use this time to heal so that you can one day open up to romantic happiness. Once you fully understand how to cope with loss, you will recognize that loss is not the end of things in life — you can get over it. Once you've worked through a major loss, you will emerge on the other side fearlessly, open to new developments and new relationships, willing to love fully and give generously. If you are not afraid of pain or grief, you will make better decisions. When you make healthy decisions, you can have stronger relationships with people who are also healthy. Facing your emotions and working through them will renew your confidence in yourself. Do the work and fight the urge to fill the vacuum with empty things or self-destructive behaviors. When you do your work to heal the pain, whilst affirming yourself, being optimistic about your future, and creating goals, you will evolve from this experience a happier, tougher, and better person. This is the work that will fix you and transform your life.

Thinking about your relationship is a necessary part of the grieving cycle, but it's also the one that can drive you mad. To let go of the bond, you need to see it for what it is. Your mind may shift into overdrive, incessantly processing through the details of the relationship. You can't help thinking about all those details. You reenact the breakup scene over and again, or you revisit the happy moments. Your mind may bounce between the breakup and the good times. The mind thinks about the person you loved and then when that person turned into the one who hurt you. The moments and dialogues flash through your mind randomly, with your feelings reacting to what's playing on the big screen in your brain. You want to shake it off, but you can't. The endless rumination may be depressing, but it's mentally important to work through it and be over it, surprisingly. This won't last forever, so that doesn't mean you won't get over it; this means you're working on getting over it.

While it may seem overwhelmingly crazy and counterproductive, constant ruminations are about letting go, not holding on. During this time, it's easy to push away thoughts and "get busy" with something else. It's good to face the sadness: write about it, pour out your thoughts in words, talk to friends and people who are interested in your well-being, stare into space, zone out, think critically about it, hate the process, but let it happen. When you start taking inventory of the relationship, you will relive the images and manage the situation. You'll still have random feelings and emotions, but until they subside, journaling serves as a good channel. Taking an inventory of the relationship puts you in control, allowing you to be the film's director.

In the journey of healing, you also need to learn how to take care of yourself. The fact is that whether a breakup makes sense to you or not, replaying the breakup and events leading to the breakup in your mind is normal. It is part of the grieving process. You have to relive all the conversations and moments to be able to make sense of them. Even though these thoughts are natural, it is very easy to lose yourself by getting obsessed. You need to know that obsession is different from reviewing the events so you can learn and grow. Obsession is when you ruminate about a situation you can't change, thinking about it over and over again looking for answers that aren't there. Obsession makes you think about an event with no positive or useful outcome. You need to ensure you aren't obsessing over your ex or the breakup. It is unhealthy. Work through it? Yes. Obsess about it? No.

Another thing you need to avoid is thinking about your mistakes. Although there might be things about you that you'd like to improve upon, that doesn't mean you're not a lovable, worthy person. Indeed, it takes being a lovable, worthy person to grow and get better. You have to decide to get back in your own head. As long as you're stuck in why, what, and how to ask and worry about what your ex is or isn't doing, you're postponing your own move forward. Certainly, if your ex has done something very out of character or against everything you believed to be true, it is hard to stop rehashing it. Combating this kind of obsession takes decision and discipline.

When you find yourself asking questions about why your ex did what he did or how you can change from who you are into someone he can love, stop yourself right there and say, "I am enough, I am loveable and I deserve to be loved." Say it as often as it takes to sink in and push out those ugly thoughts. Girl, I'm going to tell you again and again that you are enough, you are loveable, and you deserve to be loved. Don't let your mind tell you otherwise. Get in your head and change the narrative. What your ex did or didn't do no longer matters. What you could or could not have done no longer matters. What does matter is what you are doing now and that is what you should focus on.

As you are no doubt experiencing, moving on from your past relationship involves feeling and expressing pain, anger, confusion, and frustration. In addition to feeling your feelings, the road to healing includes reviewing your relationship and examining unfinished business from the past. You need to go out and meet new people, do new things, and learn a different way of being. You need to plan for the future while dealing with the present and taking a hard look at your past. All of this is difficult and demanding. The only way to stay committed to this challenging work is to balance it with positive, self-affirming actions. Not only will this solidify your commitment to the healing process, it will help keep a sense of stability in your life during this potentially unsettling time.

Throughout this process, remember that nature hates empty spaces so balance is key to everything you do. When you're doing your difficult emotional job, you have to try and make it balanced. While you're working on your emotions, you also have to take care of yourself every day, which involves recording your thoughts and feelings; affirming yourself with caring, compassionate and optimistic words; erasing your negative self-talk; making lists of all the things you are grateful for; battling obsessive thoughts; creating goals; crediting yourself and regular breaks from the work; taking out time to be physically good to yourself while also leaning on people for support.

Let's talk about journaling. While it might seem more like work than self-care, keeping a journal is one of the healing process's most vital tools. Think of your journal as a friend in a difficult time when you're trying to find an outlet to release the bad so that you can make room to take in the good. Grief is about letting out your feelings, and success is thinking positive thoughts and planning for the future. To achieve these, you need journaling. After a messy breakup, there are many things to feel, discover, think, plot, and strategize. Your journal keeps everything straight. Keeping a journal not only lets you work out what you are going through emotionally, it also helps you turn your goals and dreams into a concrete action plan. Through journaling, you describe a clear picture of what has happened in your life and what you want your future to look like, then you can plan and decide on the next thing to do. All positive change begins with an understanding of who and how you want to be. Being able to take a step back to evaluate your thoughts and feelings as well as the people around you is an effective way of controlling your life. Write your thoughts and feelings in your journal even if you don't exactly know what to make of them. Eventually these will lead you to recognize patterns in your life and notice the unresolved issues that need to be finished. Prepare to make journaling part of your daily life by thinking about the kind of journal that will best facilitate writing. Want a school notebook, an expensive leather bound diary, a special book? Will you have a journal app on your phone or laptop? Throughout the day, it can help to have a small pad or digital recorder with you to record thoughts and move them to your computer at night. Cultivate the practice and spend some time each day writing down what's going on with you and making action to move past failure. How do you feel? How are you faring? What are the things in your life that you're trying to change? It will become your second nature after a few weeks, and its effect on you will be obvious.

Now, on to positive affirmation. If you are going to heal from your past trauma, you will need to check your negative thoughts with positive affirmations. As important as it is to avoid the negative self-talk as it happens, you also need to tune in and record the daily things you say to yourself in your journal. Listen to your own thoughts and comments, then write them down. Set aside time to work with them. First, write the positive affirming words for every negative thing you say. If you catch yourself saying "I was not enough," write the exact opposite in your journal, "I am enough."

One important thing to remember when you're creating your positive affirmations is that the mind does not work in the future, it works in the present. So, instead of starting your affirmation by saying "I will be…," say "I am." Your subconscious only works with the present. While it is good to make spontaneous affirmations of encouragement whenever you have negative thoughts about yourself, it is necessary to structure the process of building your self-image. The subconscious wants constant imprinting to reprogram old ideas; here the positive affirmations make a huge difference. When you write so many affirmations, though, you dilute their strength because you can't possibly repeat that many affirmations every day. Sit down, write many proactive statements and spend time working with them to make them the best they can be. Then pick seven to twelve proactive statements to say several times a day. Cultivation must take place several times a day, every day. This may mean getting up earlier or setting aside some time at night to read them and hear what you're saying. Find a few more times a day to read or say your statements. The repetition will embed them in your subconscious.

To stop your obsessive thoughts and ruminations about your ex, replace them with something. If there's an activity you've always wanted to do or an interest you've always intended to develop, start by taking a trip to the local craft store to see if there's something you'd find interesting or absorbing. Sometimes when people feel low, they don't like to take up something challenging. Coloring may sound childish, but it is very calming. If crafts aren't for you, find something different. Read a book. Learn how to draw or knit. Learn a new language. You may want to learn coding, web design, or animation. These things require concentration and time. The exercises aim to train your brain and let it know you 're in charge. Fill your time with varied interests: cultivate a passion for art, learn languages or programming. Find something mentally challenging to do so that you don't sit around being a victim of your own mind.

Getting busy with new events is great — for a while. This kind of distraction is important to your healing process, but then it's time to retrain your brain to focus on your future. To be your own person and live your own life, it's necessary to think about your goals and how to achieve them. You know who you are, what you want, and what will make you happy. Even if you've put your dreams on a shelf or quit trying to do other things, some of you have continued to follow your dreams and still want all of these things to come true. Whether it's something big like going back to school or learning to play an instrument or learning how to save money, you have the ability to know what would make you happy. Deep down, there's a genuine self that aspires to take some time to prepare for and achieve those goals.

Goal setting works best when you break them up into long-term goals and short-term goals in different areas of your life. You won't have goals in every region, of course, but you want to choose enough different challenges to maintain your interest. Examples of goal areas are: family relationships, volunteering, philanthropy, social, culture, travel, entertainment, finance, career, education, physical, diet, exercise, and fun. Look at the list and spend some time discussing items you want to do in a few different areas. Then pick five to seven goals and determine which goal to start on first. The key to success is to make it realistic and then break it down into manageable pieces. Create a workbook that includes clear-cut strategies for short-term goals. Write down any challenges and set a completion date. Make the worksheet very specific about what steps to take to achieve your long-term target. Write about it, do your research, and find out what's best for your future. Be methodic. Don't have so many expectations so you don't get overwhelmed and can't accomplish any. Don't have goals that are unattainable and very stressful. Review your targets once a week or once a month. Give yourself plenty of praise and even small incentives to achieve your goals. Celebrate your small wins.

Your life is another vital part of this cycle. Life is what you do and make to happen not what happens to you. One way to start taking charge is to arrange regular breaks and become focused on your healing. Thinking about structuring your time can be too much during the early stages of grief. After a few weeks, it's time to put some structure into your moving-on phase. If you have an emotional day, it's okay to sob, it's okay to feel terrible for a few hours. Now it's time to take that break and do something good for yourself. Once you start doing some of the hard work we've earlier talked about, it may be tempting to try to hammer it all out in a few days, but it's easy to get inundated like that. Frequent breaks will help you find the balance you really need to recover, and help you plan a life path. Become a person responsible for your emotions and operation, instead of letting them influence you. After you've been crying for a while, it's time to get up. When you've been socializing too often and not journaling, schedule a night to be home and think about where you are now. Don't let your feelings drive you around and decide what to do.

I won't sugar coat things and tell you that the process of healing isn't hard, because it is. There are going to be times when you will break down and hate the process. It's okay to get angry or frustrated, but I need you to not give up. If you really want to build a better life for yourself after your break up, you have to dutifully follow the process. I'm sorry, there is no easy way out. But it will be worth it in the long run. You will be glad you went through the pain because you will come out a better person with a more fulfilling life.

CHAPTER SUMMARY

- To go on your journey of healing, you have to work on your past, take care of yourself in the present while planning for the future.
- To start your journey to healing, you must cut off all contact with your ex.
- You also have to take care of yourself by getting out the negative emotions and thoughts from

your past and replacing them with positive
emotions and thoughts.

- You need to take back control of your mind by
  not obsessing over your ex.
- There are a few tools to help on this journey
  including: journaling, positive self-affirmation,
  and goal setting.

IN THE NEXT chapter you will learn the different reasons
why going back to your ex is a wrong move.

CHAPTER TWO: NO, YOU DON'T NEED HIM

I t happens. Either you're going to entertain the idea or actually fall for someone who made you feel like they're the one. Sometimes, it happens. You meet a person, you get to know them, feelings spring up all over your heart and you begin to imagine a future with that person. It happens to the best of us. Then things start to change, that sense of security starts to fade. As the relationship continues, you find yourself struggling to stay afloat on a slowly sinking boat. You begin to plug the gaps with denial. You tell yourself that all is well, you make excuses for the way you're treated by this guy. You start losing yourself because you're more concerned about holding on to someone who doesn't seem to want to hold you anymore. This may have happened to you once before, maybe twic, but more likely it was more often than that. You're giving your all and yet this person makes you feel like it's not enough. You are battling again. You battle a little more before you realize that you are the only one in the fight.

You try to hold on to a failing relationship due to the time you spent in it. You are staying for the energy you gave.

You're staying because you're holding on to any hoped-for potential they'll be the person they promised to be. They apologize in an effort to manipulate you into thinking they're all you deserve. You want all these things. You want love, you want comfort, you want passion, you want them to be considerate in their care for you, and yet you get to the point where you realize that you have been searching for all of these qualities in the wrong person. Yeah, there are good moments, good memories, some here and there but all you can think about is how hurt you are. All you can think about is how much you get hurt as you sit, waiting for them to mess up again. That's no way to live; you're dead, buried alive in a grave that's become your relationship.

Then the breakup comes. Finally, you've built up enough courage to walk away or the person you're holding on to decides to walk away from you to find someone else to use and even so, it's done in a way that makes you question your own worth. It is an awful thing to experience. Feeling that you're no longer good enough for the person who pretended you're all they ever needed, but was trying to get what they wanted from you. You are probably still trying to work out this pain within you that makes you feel like you're never going to be good enough.

I am going to be sincere with you and tell you that even after all the work you've done, there are still times when you'll desperately want to get back with your ex. You are human and this is totally natural. It's okay to miss him or even want him back after everything that happened. It doesn't make you an idiot. The fact is that some people have broken up and gotten back together and the relationship still worked out. More often than not, these relationships still end in heartbreaks. The point is: getting back together with your ex is a horrible idea. Yes, it might look like things will be different this time, he might even vow that he is a changed person. Believe me, 90 percent of the time, it'll still end in heartbreak.

When you go back to someone who mistreated you, you 're cheating yourself out of the chance to be with someone who will always take your feelings into consideration. If you go back to him, you might never find the happiness you want. Don't go back to those things your emotional strength no longer needs. Sometimes exes are a major distraction from the things that we truly deserve in life. You really do not need him in your life. Look at all the progress you have made so far. Why would you want to jeopardize that for a chance to get back with someone you're better off without? I've come to realize that there are a lot of materials out there that talk about how to get your ex back, how to make your ex come back begging, how to make him love you forever. The fact remains that you are better off without him. Why you broke up doesn't matter. The fact that you broke up is enough. Let's go through a few reasons why you should not get back together with your ex.

PEOPLE NEVER REALLY CHANGE

So, he has promised to change, and maybe even said he has changed. Face the fact: people never really change. A leopard never changes his spots. People can be incredible talkers. To say it, and indeed to do it, are two entirely different things. If you're hearing lots of talk about how much they've changed from who you knew, look for the proof. Talk is cheap. For example, if your ex expresses to you how trustworthy they have become, watch how they act when they explain them-selves to you. Is their attitude and conduct trustworthy? Or do they screen messages and skip details of what they've been up to recently? In short, if what your ex does is not in align-ment with what they're saying, they probably haven't changed. Think about what he was like when you decided to break up with him. Have you gotten the picture? That's exactly what he still is. If he's begging you to come back, you should expect him to tell you what you want to hear which is the fact that he has changed. Look, you can't take the risk of letting him back into your life only to find out that he is still the same jerk you dumped. You know what's going to happen if you let him back into your life? He's going to pretend to be a better person for as long as he can keep up the pretense. Then when he let's go of the façade, you'll realize that he's still the exact same person you dumped. Then you'll blame yourself for going back to him. You'll face the same issues that made you leave him in the first place. Your self-esteem will take a serious blow and you'll be back to where you were. Now, you'll have to start working on your emotional healing and getting over him all over again. We really do not want this. So, sweetheart, block his number, block him on Instagram and twitter and move on with your life. Why? Because you don't need him.

THE RELATIONSHIP WAS TOXIC

If you broke up with him because the relationship was toxic and unhealthy, why do you want to go back to him? Because you think things will be different this time? Sweetheart, things are still going to be the same. He will still exhibit those same behaviors that made you feel like you don't deserve to be loved. He will still talk to you in the same condescending manner, he will still make you feel stupid, he will still make you feel like your emotions don't matter, or that you are too sensitive while he is saying hurtful things. He hasn't changed and won't change. You really do not want to keep being this guy's victim. Still need more convincing? Sit down and think back on when you were still with him. Think about how he used to make you feel. The hurt, the confusion, the inferiority complex, how he made you feel like you were crazy, the unhappiness. Going back to him will bring all of these back. It might not be immediate, but when the "honeymoon" period is over, guess who is going to be plunged back into all of that. Look, you deserve to be happy. You are an amazing sweetheart. You deserve love that doesn't come with pain. You deserve every good thing. But this guy can't give them to you. If you search deep down, and put aside the sentiments, you'll see that this guy is bad news and the best place you can be is away from him.

YOU WERE HIS SIDE CHICK

So, you broke up with him after finding out you were his side chick. Now he's back with the story that he never loved his main girlfriend and has broken up with her to be with you. Lies! Lies! Lies! This guy was never sincere from the beginning and you think he's going to start now? He's out to play Russian Roulette with your heart and emotions. He had a main girlfriend and made you think you were his only girlfriend. Not only was he unfaithful to you, he was unfaithful to the other woman. Now, you're thinking of going back to a guy that cheated on two women at the same time? Really? And you think he'll be faithful to you this time? Avoid wasting your time with this jerk. He's not worth a second though from you. Chances are, this guy is still with his girlfriend and wants you back as his side chick, or he wants you to be his main girlfriend while he has yet another side chick. Don't fall for his lies. They are nothing more than that: lies. You deserve to be with a guy who will be faithful to you. You deserve to be loved without having to fight for it. You are worth more than being only a side chick. You should be the center of a guy's world and not a side attraction. Again, I'm telling you that you don't need him.

HE IS ABUSIVE

I know it's normal to want to go back to your ex even though he was abusive because you keep remembering the picture of him when he was loving, doting, and caring. You keep thinking back on the times when things were rosy, the times before he became abusive. You think it's okay to go back to him because things will be different this time. You think he was abusive because you provoked him. You think if you can change into a better version of yourself, the abuse will stop. First I need you to know that the abuse wasn't your fault whether it was physical or emotional abuse. You didn't provoke it and there was nothing you could have done to stop it. Honestly, these days, getting out of an abusive relationship alive is a feat. Why would you want to go back? Especially when your ex hasn't even realized that there is something wrong with him and isn't getting any help. You shouldn't put your life at risk like that. Abuse is a serious issue. You could lose your mind or even your life by staying in an abusive relationship. You were lucky enough to get out once and now you're thinking of going back? Don't. You are doing fine without him and someday, you'll meet someone who will love you without hurting you. You are worthy of love.

YOUR EX IS SELFISH AND ONLY CARES ABOUT HIS SELFISH NEEDS

I know I don't have to spell it out to you because you know your ex is a very selfish person. Maybe he was only with you because he had a need you were meeting, but he didn't really care about you. There are relationships where the ladies are the ones feeding the guy. When they eventually decide to break up, the guy starts begging them to come back. Not because he loves her, but because he needs her to provide money for him to live on. Sometimes, it could even be sex. Your ex might be begging you to come back, not because he loves you, but because you are good in bed. I can imagine how miserable the relationship was for you. And now you want to go back because he has been saying he can't live without you. Guess what? If you don't go back, he won't die and he will find someone else to meet his selfish needs because he was only using you and never really loved you. You don't need someone like that in your life. Block his number.

YOUR EX IS A LIAR

So, your ex is a lying jerk. He was never honest about things. He is the kind of person that would lie to your face about something you both could see and then make you feel like you weren't seeing the situation properly. Now, he wants you back and, let me guess, he's still denying ever having lied to you. This kind of behavior in people can make you feel like you are a crazy person who is always accusing them of things they didn't do, and that they are, in fact, angels. Look, if you want to spend another long year calling out his lying ass and feeling like you are the crazy person, then go ahead and get back together with him. When you finally decide to dump his ass, you'll spend years trying to get over the damage he did to you. You are better off without him because he's never going to change. Nothing you do will make him stop lying. You are going back to the place where you catch him in a lie and he still lies to cover up. This guy is a serial liar. You already made a good decision by breaking up with him. Don't go back.

Unless you want to go back to being labeled "the crazy girlfriend."

YOU STILL HAVE UNRESOLVED ISSUES

Think about it. You broke up because you had a lot of issues. Maybe he wasn't a bad person, but the two of you still had issues you couldn't get past. If you get back together, the relationship still won't work out because you haven't resolved those issues. You will still have the same issues that caused you to break up. I get that you feel like you might be missing out on being with an amazing person, but there are amazing people out there that you haven't met yet. If your ex has not learned much from your last relationship, or has not taken the time to develop as a person and as a partner, chances are you may have some of the same problems as the last time. Say, for example, your ex was continually moaning about their miserable work situation in your first relationship with each other, and refused to do anything about it. If your ex does have the same career, or still refuses to actively change their future, you will still experience the same frustrations together. If your ex hasn't matured as an adult, then when you decide to try again, you're bound to run into similar issues in your relationship. It's best not to relive past aggravations by giving your ex another chance. If you don't want to go back to a miserable relationship, then stay away from him. Someone better will come along and you may not have so many issues.

IF HE DID IT ONCE, HE WILL DO IT AGAIN

We humans are creatures of habit. Whatever he did that made you break up with him, he will do it again. If he hit you, he will hit you again. If he cheated on you, he will cheat again. People never really change. You might be thinking it was a mistake to break up. It was not. He has always had that behavior in him and he got the perfect avenue to act it out. What's to say he won't do it again? Don't set yourself up for pain again by going back to him. He's in your past now and you should only be looking forward. Let him go. Tell him, "Bye!" and move forward.

HE DOESN'T RESPECT YOU

If your ex was that guy that never had an iota of respect for you, why do you think going back to him is a good idea? He was disrespectful, demeaning, and condescending. He made you feel like your opinion doesn't matter. He made you feel stupid or that didn't measure up to him. He crushed your self-esteem. You probably feel like you can't do better than him. That's not true. You can do a lot better than him. You need to work on yourself and you'll find someone better than him. You need to get rid of what years of his disrespect did to you. You need to take back the space he rented in your head, and when you do, you will flourish.

TRUST WAS A HUGE PROBLEM

Think about it: you broke up with this guy because you found out he was cheating or told a major lie or told many lies. Your trust in him was shattered. Maybe he wasn't truthful throughout the length of your relationship. Now, he says he's sorry and wants you to come back. In every relationship, trust is a major pillar but you no longer trust this guy. Can't you see you'll be setting yourself up for heartache and disappointment if you go back to him? Every time he comes home late or doesn't even show up, you'll start wondering where he is, who he's with and what he's doing. Every time you see a call from someone you don't know, you'll start wondering who it is and whether he's cheating on you. Every time things don't seem to add up, you'll start wondering if he has been lying to you. Sweetheart, you don't need all of this. You are better off without him.

HE DUMPED YOU FOR SOMEONE ELSE

I simply cannot understand why you would want to go back to someone who dumped you. Whatever excuse you might want to give yourself isn't plausible. You deserve better. I really cannot stress it enough: you deserve better. If you need some motivation to not go back to him, think about how you felt when he dumped you, then think about how you felt when you found out that he actually dumped you for someone else. It hurt, didn't it? Now, that's the motivation you need to tell him to get lost. If he could hurt you like that, then he didn't deserve you when you were together the first time, let alone deserving a second chance. Make all the excuses you can for him. I give you permission. Write them down if you have to. Now, read through them again and tell yourself that no excuse is reason enough for you to go back. He shouldn't even be able to contact you, so he won't even have the opportunity of asking you to come back. Unapologetically block his number!

IT WAS A REALLY UGLY BREAKUP

Think about how things ended with your ex. Did he break up with a text? Did he give you a valid reason? Did he walk out on the relationship? Or did he break up with a flimsy excuse. This says a lot about the kind of guy he is and what he really thought of you. A reasonable breakup is one where you both sit down and talk about why the relationship has to end and why you are better off apart. When he called off everything without a solid reason, and even mocked you or blamed it on you, he shows that he doesn't value you. Why would you want to get back with someone who has no or little regard for you and abandons you over a single text? Treat yourself better and stop thinking about getting back with him. He's not worth your time, let alone your heart.

YOU ARE LONELY

After a breakup, you're very fragile. You spent so much time with someone else. Having that human contact and then being suddenly left all alone can leave you feeling empty. You 're going through a withdrawal. When this happens, taking your ex back can be an easy way out without really thinking about it. Do you really miss him? Without him, is your life really worse? Or are you just lonely? Think of your desires. Wanting to get your ex back and wanting to touch somebody are two different things. Even if you're not yet over your ex, you are still better off without him. Getting back with him because you're lonely and crave human contact will definitely result in the same problems that split you two up in the first place. The best option for you at this point is to be gainfully occupied. Don't go back to him.

YOU MIGHT LOSE YOUR FRIENDS

This depends in particular on the number of chances you have already given your ex. Remember that your friends are often the ones who hear all the awful things about your ex during and after your relationship. Most likely your friends will try to talk to you about not giving your ex another chance, particularly if they realize that your ex doesn't deserve you. If you ignore their honest advice and go ahead and take your ex back, then your friends will get upset. Only in extreme cases will your friends actually give up on you. More frequently, when you give your ex a fourth or fifth chance to convince you that "things are going to be different," abandonment happens. You should trust the decisions of your mates, they know you and they stuck with you through your relationships and know what's all right and what isn't. If your friends really matter to you, then rethink your decision to give your ex another chance. Your friends are humans and there's only so much they can take. When he dumps you again, you'll still come and dump your emotional baggage on them. At a point it gets tiring. Stop giving him extra chances.

YOU DON'T WANT THE SAME THING

If your life goals and desires are not compatible with your ex's and you want to give them another shot, you will most likely run into problems again. You both need to be on the same page, or at least the same chapter, when you are sharing your life with someone else. To support each other fully, you both need to understand the goals and dreams of the other, and help each other achieve them. If your ex doesn't support your life goals, be they career, family or personal, you shouldn't give your ex another opportunity. A relationship should involve support for each other. If he isn't on the same page with you, or you with him, then there is absolutely no point in getting back together. You are going to end up resenting him because he doesn't seem to be interested in supporting your dreams. In cases like this, it's best you guys don't get back together.

HE PROBABLY HAS NEW, MORE DISGUSTING HABITS

When we love somebody, we seem to let them off the hook for their nasty and annoying habits that would otherwise make us heave silently. Habits like failing endlessly to flush the toilet or not putting the cap back on the toothpaste. I don't know what odd habits your exes have, but I'm sure they're many. Oh, over time those little habits may have gotten worse, or weirder. Or perhaps, in your first relationship, you never noticed them, and now you find yourself being exposed to a variety of disturbing and appalling habits that you would rather live without. You have no idea what new annoying habit he has picked up and you most certainly do not want to find out. You really got off the annoying train and want to get back on it? Save yourself the headache and let bygones be bygones.

YOU'VE MADE IT THROUGH ALREADY

Hello, look in the mirror at that person? Simple! You still breathe; your life is not over. You 're past the finish line in your healing; why turn around and do it all over again by getting back together with you ex? The only one you lose on returning to your ex is you. You're wasting money, incentives, and doors opening on new opportunities all to end up where you started. Do you really want to undo all the progress you've made? It's going to be a whole lot of wasted efforts. All I'm saying is: you already cried about the break up, you did the work and made it through, you've been making so much progress and now you want to go back? Tell you what, you are going to be back to the breakup stage and start all over again. It's not fair on you. Don't go back.

No matter how you look at this, even if you look at it from a thousand points of views, getting back with your ex is still a terrible idea. I don't want you to come back to this book in months with a fresh heartbreak wishing you had listened to my advice. Getting back together with this guy is nothing but bad news. If you search deep down, you already know what's going to happen. You already know it won't work and you'll end up broken again. This might sound harsh, but you need to block him on all social media. Block his number, block him on Facebook, Instagram, Twitter, block him everywhere. It might look petty, but it is a sure way to stop him from contacting you to spew his lies. Think about all the things you stand to lose if you go back to him. Everybody in your life knows he treated you like trash and they sure would not want you two getting back together. Now, what will you tell your family and friends if you guys get back together? Think of how stupid you will look to them. Think of how disappointed they will be because they know you deserve better and can certainly do better than him.

Apart from all of this, really think about yourself. What will your life be like if you go back to him? Will you be happy with him? Will you return to walking on eggshells around him? Will you return to taking the disrespect he throws at you? Worst of all, if he is abusive, will you make it out of the relationship alive this time? Don't you think you deserve better? Even if you don't think so, I know you deserve better. I'm telling you right now that you deserve better. Don't go back to him. Your past is your past for a reason. Let it stay there. Some people don't realize what they have until it's gone, but that doesn't always mean they should get it back. There is a reason why he is your ex. Taking the time to really understand these reasons will make it clear that you shouldn't get back together with him. Avoid getting wrapped up in what you think you want, and concentrate on what you need. Whatever you decide to do, however, forgiveness is always required. Forgiveness allows you to heal so that your next significant other will not become your next ex.

Chapter Summary

- Getting back with your ex might be the most horrible decision you'll ever make.
- You are better off without him.
- He doesn't deserve you.
- If he couldn't keep you when he had the chance, why should you go back to him now?

In the next chapter you will see why you are better off being single and why you should enjoy being single.

CHAPTER THREE: WHO NEEDS A BOYFRIEND, ANYWAY?

You have decided not to take your ex back. Let's now talk about the fact that you are better off being single. Society should not dictate important decisions in your life. This power resides with you and you alone. Nobody should pressure you into living a life you are not cut out for or interested in living.

Being single has a whole range of psychological advantages, according to a report by the University of California, Santa Barbara. Bella DePaulo, a social psychologist, has examined 814 married and single-person studies and her results are very significant. She found that single people were more self-reliant and inspired than those people in couples. Singles were also more likely to develop as individuals and meet personal goals they set in relationships faster than those paired off. Single people also have stronger relationships with their parents, family, friends, and colleagues. In addition, she found married people likely to be more unsociable. Moreover, during her presentation at the conference of the American Psychological Association, her study demonstrated that being married as well as being single, often has advantages.

"Americans can pursue the livelihoods that work best for them more than ever before. There's no blueprint for a good life," said Bella. "What matters is not what everyone else is doing or what they think we should be doing, but how we can find the places, the spaces, and the people that suit who we really are and make us live our best lives."

Being single is not a bad thing, no matter what our culture might tell you. In reality, more and more people are actively choosing to remain single because they are genuinely content with being alone. In reality, not everyone is meant for married life – there are those of us who are better off single. Bella also noted that single life provides an opportunity for people to live their best, most honest, most meaningful lives.

The traditional view celebrates and encourages marriage, while singles are attacked, judged, and abused as selfish and alienated individuals. Contrary to this assumption, there is no isolation between single individuals and their loved ones. They're probably more loyal to their families, friends, and colleagues than married couples are.

That is because, according to Bella, when people get married they no longer have time or interest in interacting with and engaging in the lives of others. In addition, the research that compared married people with those who remained single indicates that single life gives individuals a greater sense of self-worth and self-determination. She hopes that more and more people will understand the inaccuracy and narrow-mindedness of the popular assumption that marriage is the primary source for happiness and well-being. Besides, being single is not so easy, too. Single people also face challenges as much as they enjoy the advantages of being single. For example, do they remain single by choice or are there other factors. Besides addressing the clichés that come with choosing this kind of lifestyle, they even lose out on great benefits from the government.

It is now the 21st Century. It is truly your choice at the end of the day and we live in an era when it's okay to choose to be single. So, choose wisely and do what will make you happy and fulfilled. I'm going to walk you through some advantages of being single.

YOU MAY BE CARRYING TOO MUCH EMOTIONAL BAGGAGE

Most times people jump into another relationship right after a messy breakup. They don't allow themselves to sort through all the negative emotions they are carrying from the last relationship. Now in a new relationship, they find out that things are unusually hard. They can't show emotions, can't be vulnerable around their new partner, and they can't love him, no matter how hard they try. If you're unable to manifest something you desire, like love, it's sometimes because you still retain so much negative emotion towards it. If you remain single long enough to process your feelings and thoughts about past relationships, you will attract and commit yourself completely to a caring, lasting relationship with a new individual. Being single gives you the necessary time that allows you to get over the pain and emotional trauma of your last relationship.

YOU CAN SPEND THE ENTIRE DAY BINGE WATCHING MOVIES WITH COMPLETE FREEDOM

We all know we have days when we want to curl up on our couch and binge watch our favourite TV series and you remember how your ex used to complain about it. Yeah, you get to miss that. When you're single, nobody complains when you indulge yourself. It is now solely your life and you do not need to bother anybody else. You can spend the whole day on your couch, only getting up to grab a snack and nobody gets mad at you for it. When you're in a relationship, especially when you live together, you don't get to enjoy this freedom.

BEING SINGLE ALLOWS YOU TO EXPLORE

There are so many different ways to interpret the world "explore." Being single gives you a taste of the many different opportunities life has to offer: the freedom to date socially without commitment; the freedom to travel around the world; the freedom to engage in encouraging personal growth. You get to do all the things you've always wanted to do without the constraint of a relationship. Think of all the things you wanted to do when you were with your ex. Now is the time to actually do them. It also eliminates the chance of becoming resentful if you want to leave the single life behind, or when you do. It's time to date that guy who caught your eye, to take that trip you've always wanted to take, to enrol in the yoga or meditation class. Whatever crazy idea you've had in your head, now is the time to go for it. Live life to the fullest.

SINGLE PEOPLE ARE HEALTHIER

There's some evidence that shows that single individuals get more exercise than married ones. According to a report published in the Journal of Marriage and Family, divorced people are getting more exercise than married people, but those who have always been single are the ones who are most involved in their physical activity.

In a blog article for Psychology Today, social psychologist Bella DePaulo explains how women who have always been single are happier overall than women who are currently married, and they often have fewer days of sickness and fewer visits to doctors. The research, published in Social Science & Medicine, found that singles in nine European countries had a lower BMI than married couples, and weighed around five pounds less overall.

YOUR FRIENDSHIPS WILL FLOURISH

A research article published in the journal showed that people who have always been single were more attentive to their friends and relatives than married people are. Bella DePaulo wrote about this in another blog post where she says with couples it isn't just a case of infatuation in the first few months but it's going to be a continual issue of isolation. Single people also have a wider range of people they regard as close friends. They have apparently put more work into maintaining good sibling relationships. Single people value their friendships as well as relationships with their family because they don't think their lives revolve around a man. Think about it. You get to work on your friendships when you don't spend all your time on only one person. Attached people prefer to stay in the bubbles of relationships. When you're single, it's about enlarging your social circle. Even a chemistry-less date has the potential to become a good friendship.

BEING SINGLE GIVES YOU THE OPPORTUNITY TO REFLECT, THINK, AND DISCOVER YOURSELF

Giving yourself some time can be seen as an opportunity to get to know who you are again and what you really need. If you've been hurt in the past, you may be tempted to rush into a new relationship with someone that is wrong for you because you're trying to subconsciously heal the pain you're feeling. When you take time to be single, you will realize that time is a great healer. You learn to let go of your past instead of falling into repeat addiction - going from relationship to relationship to avoid the pain of each breakup. Simultaneously, you should discover new places and seek new things and find out who you are and what kind of person a perfect match for you would be. One of the most important relationships you will have is with yourself. Being single can be a great opportunity to learn about your likes and dislikes, to accept your true self, and to pursue hobbies or activities that you have been itching to try out. Your last partner may have hated running and you have always wanted to attempt a marathon.Maybe you've dreamed of traveling to Hawaii, but you've been waiting for a buddy to share those intimate beach massages with. Instead, accept and embrace your self-reliance. You're going to learn to value your freedom, make your own decisions, and become more accountable for your choices, actions, and goals. People who can make their own decisions, choose when and how they grow their own inner power and who they share it with. Remember: No spouse "completes" you. You've got to be a single, happy person on your own before sharing your life with another.

THERE IS LESS HOUSE WORK

If you had a live-in boyfriend, then being single can be a breath of fresh air. Do you hate chores? Then being single is a right choice. Having a live-in boyfriend requires seven additional hours a week of women's housework, according to a survey. Women who live with their man have done more housework than those who remained single. If you have a partner to satisfy, leaving dirty dishes in the sink doesn't work. So, being single gives you the liberty to do your dishes whenever you feel like it without someone complaining about how untidy the kitchen looks. You get to leave your laundry in the basket for days without folding it and putting it away and nobody complains.

YOU HAVE FEWER CONFLICTS

No one enjoys conflict, but if you are extremely uncomfortable with confrontation, it may be advantageous to remain single for your psychological well-being. Individuals who are conflict-averse (meaning relationship fights and arguments cause them extreme stress) will feel less anxious when they're single, according to a report. If you're someone that hates conflicts or confrontations, you will flourish being single. Relationships come with a lot of conflicts and confrontations. Additionally, you'll be spared the frustration of dealing with annoying habits, allowing you to concentrate on getting rid of your own. You don't need to nag anyone to wash the dishes or take out the trash because you're going to take responsibility for routine tasks. If you like to disagree with only yourself aloud, yet another advantage of living alone is that it will mentally save you from the disagreements, arguments, heartbreaks, and outbursts that surround relationships. Yes of course, the honeymoon period of a relationship appears fun, and all but it is almost impossible to stop the occasional bickering. Flying solo means avoiding arguments about where to go for dinner or who skipped ahead on that television show you should be watching together. Singles get to enjoy and eat whatever their heart desires — without fear of having to share the final slice or piece. To be single is to have fewer conflicts.

YOU GET THE CHANCE AND TIME TO FIND YOURSELF

Some people identify themselves by who their partner is. They adopt the interests of their lover, and they always think of themselves as a couple. Does that sound familiar to you? If you've forgotten who you are while you're in the relationship universe, then it's time to find yourself again. It's time to remind yourself of who you are and what you stand for. Or if you feel like you no longer know who that is, you can start from scratch. And it's all better to do when you're single. You don't have to adopt his way of life, thinking it's yours. One of the major reasons why you should remain single is so you can find yourself and define who you are, as well as define what your values and belief system is, instead of living someone else's life. Being single gives you the chance to think about yourself and feel happier, which would instantly become evident to others and make you more appealing to them. Don't fall for the idea that you need someone else to tell you how wonderful you are. Being single opens your schedule and mind, creating space for you to figure out who you want to be and the best way to do so. Nobody else around you is asking for your attention, so go out there and become that woman. You get to use your time the way you want to. During busy days at work or in school, there is no one to fight with you because you can't give time to your outings or late night calls.

BEING SINGLE GRANTS YOU FREEDOM

It's also important to remember that there are pros and cons to being in a committed relationship. The spontaneity open to you as a single person is not to be taken for granted. You can spend your money however you want, live as you like, book last minute vacations, and create your schedule solely according to what you like. This is a time in your life when it's necessary to simply enjoy the freedom, lest you regret giving it up too quickly. For starters, single life awards you more flexibility and independence. You have to answer to no one but yourself, you get to avoid uncomfortable compromise and emotional conflict. You will have to cook and clean for yourself, of course, but you alone can select the menu according to your preferences, and you will set your own standards. You will enjoy your leisure time by discovering new things that you will enjoy and that will, in turn, make you a more attractive person to others and a better friend. It is not selfish to do things for yourself that you are free to do. What is selfish is to limit someone else's freedom by binding them to you when you cannot reciprocate entirely. The single life gives you greater control of your time, which you can spend in so many ways like exercising or volunteering at your local library or at a shelter helping those less fortunate than yourself. Alternatively, you may spend time improving your career, going back to school, or caring for relatives.

Being single gives you the right to do what you want (unless you're still living under your parents' home roof). You are not responsible to any partner and nobody is entitled to tell you what to do or not to do. You can dye your hair pink, get a tattoo, spend or save your money on anything you want — and nobody's going to get angry with you. The possibilities are endless. Enjoy the single life.

YOU CAN KEEP AS MANY PETS AS YOU WANT

If you're a lady with three cats and the kids in the neighbourhood have begun to call you the cat lady, that's great. Fill your house with as many dogs and cats as you wish. Adopt a bird for a little excitement in the mix! A hamster, a ferret, even a mouse: you can have all. You have to be able to take care of them. Nobody complains about your pet because you're not sharing your space with anybody. Also, since you don't have a partner, nobody nags about having to help you take care of them. You can do whatever you want. You can even let your dog hop in bed with you. This is really the time to unleash your inner animal person.

YOU CAN HAVE MALE FRIENDS AND IT'S OKAY

I think it is appropriate for married people to have friends of the opposite sex. A good opposite-sex friend can give insight and help in ways that are often completely underestimated, particularly to married folks. I think the reason why people are so reluctant to forge these friendships is that even some singles wonder if it's okay to have opposite sex friendships when you're in a relationship. The key is to remember that a true friend will respect boundaries, will honour your relationship and will do all they can to make your significant other feel as comfortable as possible. Unfortunately, a lot of people in relationships don't see it this way. As a result, they have no opposite sex friends and their partner (at least to the best of their knowledge) does not do so either. You have to respect that when you're married. You can call and hang out with whoever you want while you're single. The friendships you have are your business. There's no need to run it by your boyfriend. When you're single, you can spend as much time with a male friend as you do a female friend without someone asking questions or getting jealous.

YOU GET TO TRY OUT NEW HOBBIES

When you're single, the universe is your playground. Those hobbies you have been itching to try? It's time to sign up for the class. When you are in a serious relationship, you are not completely cut off from the world, but let's face it: it's easy to get caught up in a rut of movie nights and dinner dates. Now that you are single, you get to make use of all your solitary time and broaden your personal horizon. Relationships demand a lot of time investments and this can make you drop some of your interests so you can focus on building a relationship. Being single allows you the liberty to invest in your hobbies without worrying about not spending enough time with your partner. It is time to indulge yourself and try out new hobbies.

YOU DON'T HAVE TO WONDER WHETHER YOU ARE WITH THE RIGHT PERSON

Being in a relationship can make you ask a lot of questions. Questions like: Am I with the right person? Does he really love me? How do I know if what I feel for him is love? This can be overwhelming especially when the relationship looks like it's heading towards marriage. Nobody wants to marry the wrong person. When you're single, however, you don't have to wonder if you're with the right person. The only thing you have to worry about is what you'll have for dinner.

YOU DON'T HAVE TO WORRY ABOUT BEING CHEATED ON

The freedom of being single brings the benefit of knowing that nobody cheats you. That feeling may sound a little sad on the surface but it really isn't. Relationships aren't for everybody, and much of life's suffering comes from having to force yourself into circumstances that you shouldn't necessarily be in. Being single brings a degree of security to your life where you are insulated from the harsh notion of investing your time and heart into someone who turns around with their infidelity and stabs you in the back. Really, being single helps you sleep better at night because you won't be up wondering if your boyfriend is cheating on you. You don't have to be suspicious of every girl you see with your boyfriend. It allows you a lot of peace. Being cheated on is not a nice experience. It can leave you feeling like you weren't enough for him or that maybe there's something wrong with you. While all these feelings are wrong, it's better to not put yourself in that situation. Being single can be a luxury, depending on how you look at it.

THERE'S NO REASON TO HAVE SECOND THOUGHTS ABOUT STUDYING ABROAD

When you are in a relationship you can no longer afford to make impulsive choices. Whether you like it or not, your partner has a say in any big decision you need to make, such as living overseas, moving to another city, or transitioning in your career. Being single gives you the absolute power to determine your future for yourself. We all know what it's like to have to take your boyfriend into consideration before making any major decision. You have second thoughts about studying abroad because you don't want to leave him behind or because you don't trust him to be faithful while you're away. When you are single, you don't have to worry about any of these scenarios. You can take that admission offer to study or work in another country and not be scared of losing anybody. You can focus on your studies or your work because you don't have to keep a steady relationship. My best friend, who is a guy, once broke up with a girl he really liked. When I asked him why, guess what the reason was? He broke up with her because he was investing a lot of time and effort in the relationship and he wanted to focus on graduating from school and attaining financial stability. It's high time we ladies started thinking like this. If a guy could break up with a girl he liked to focus on his education, then how much better will it be when you are single?

YOUR BANK ACCOUNT WILL FLOURISH

It's a fallacy to say that people with partners are financially better off. While couples can share certain costs, it doesn't put single people at a disadvantage. Indeed, being single can be a huge benefit. When you're single, you're never going to have to clear any ideas with your partner and you're never going to have to compromise, which makes choices much easier and allows for extra savings. There are many benefits to being single, and many go beyond the obvious. If you're worried about being alone, look at all the ways it can actually make your life better. There are some incredible opportunities, even though it may be hard at first. You can save much more for yourself if you're not going on dates. Everyone would certainly agree that being single can help you stick to your budget better. Also, if you're single, you don't have to worry about buying gifts for a partner, particularly on Valentine's, Christmas, or birthdays. Single people are less likely to have credit card debt, coming in at around 21 percent, according to a Debt.com survey. On the other hand, 27 percent of married couples without children had credit card debt as do 36 percent of married couples with children. Financial debt will affect your health tremendously, including placing you at a greater risk of heart attacks, strokes, and high blood pressure.

YOU ARE BOUND TO ADVANCE IN YOUR CAREER

There are several variables that go into how happy you are at work, and without a partner you are more free to follow your career choices without restrictions. You don't have to ask what your partner thinks you should do, if they would be willing to relocate to a different city to follow you for a great opportunity, or whether you think the job you really want is going to pay enough to evenly distribute the financial weight in the partnership. Research suggests that singles may enjoy their 9-to-5 more because they value meaningful work more than married people do. Having the ability to log long hours will definitely pay off if your purpose is to rapidly climb the corporate ladder. If you want to rise to the top of the pack -- even higher than the boys, staying single early in your career might be a sensible decision. A 2010 study showed that young, childless, unwed women earned an average of 15 percent more than their male counterparts in big cities like New York and LA in certain job markets, and that success would later lead to a boost in attitude. Focusing on career over relationships allows more energy and mental space to climb the ladder -- and that doesn't mean you're never going to tie the knot. Research shows women who are highly educated tend to get married and reproduce later in life. So, take the time to set up yourself in the 20s and early 30s. Being single helps you to focus and do better in your career, since there is no distraction in the form of trying to maintain a steady relationship.

YOU ARE COMPLETELY IN CONTROL OF YOUR HAPPINESS

Indeed, the stress of problematic relationships often stems from the misplaced expectations that you and your partner should do things to make the other happy, says Wasson. If you're unattached, you avoid this trap because you know unless you don't try to make the other person happy, it won't happen. Since singles become more aware of their needs, they develop the resources to create their own happiness. This can be frustrating in the short run because, yes, it would be good to be able to fall back on a partner. But since singles tend to develop the resources to create their own happiness, it will be invaluable in future for healthy relationships if they decide to couple up.

YOU SLEEP BETTER

Cuddling is great and all but if your boyfriend disturbs your sleep due to a sleeping disorder, a different bedtime, or by tossing and turning all night, it can seriously mess your sleep up. "People with obstructive sleep apnea can make a lot of noise and are very restless which can disturb their partner," says Steven Scharf M.D., Ph.D., director of the Sleep Disorders Centre at the University of Maryland. There is also intermittent limb movement disorder (where one flails around in their sleep), REM behavioural disorder (which involves "acting out" dreams), sleep walking, night terrors — the list goes on. "In many situations, couples in these circumstances end up in different bedrooms at night because one of them cannot sleep," Scharf says. Not only can you sleep in your own bed if you're single, but you get the countless health benefits that come with eight solid hours a night.

YOU GET TO HAVE MORE SEX WITHOUT STRINGS ATTACHED

Single people have sex more often than married people do according to an analysis of survey data collected from over 26,000 people. I remember this girl who told me about an experience when she met this man who she thought was super-hot. The first day they met they had sex. She said it was good but not the best she had had. She had recently broken up with her boyfriend so she was not looking for a relationship. She just wanted to have fun and she continued to see this man. They always hooked up for sex. Over time, they started having conversations and the sex started getting better. This arrangement continued for almost two years. She was getting satisfied sexually and also had time to focus on other things. It was better than getting a boyfriend. She got to have regular sex without complications that come with relationships. Being single affords you the liberty to have sex as much as you want without strings attached and without commitment as long as the arrangement is consensual for both people.

An increasing number of people across the globe have chosen to be single. According to the United States Census Bureau, the number of American women who have never been married or divorced and live alone has been on an upward trajectory for many years. I believe it is the same in other parts of the world, because women are starting to realize the benefits of being single and also because women have the financial means to do so.

Dr. Elyakim Kislev, a professor at Jerusalem's Hebrew University, found that if you're single, you can redefine the term for yourself: You don't have to be lonely, so you're not a loser. He believes being single can be an asset, rather than a cause of pain. Kislev analysed US and European databases and conducted interviews to examine lifestyle trends and what made some singles happy, finding that happiness was a lifestyle choice for some, or something they came to accept.

Some happy singles found pleasure in their choice, reinforced by participating in new and exciting experiences, such as traveling or discovering new hobbies, experiences that would have otherwise been hard to explore while in a relationship. They used their time alone to build themselves up and be motivated in the moment by concentrating on themselves, Kislev said.

Others were satisfied because they deliberately built robust social networks as alternatives to intimate romantic relations. They invited their friends to join them on more outings, spent more time talking to their neighbours, and kept in closer touch with their families. The results found that up to 45 per cent more single individuals socialized with their friends than their married counterparts. Singles have more friends than married people on average. There is a pattern in which married people turn inward and neglect their friends and family. Instead, singles cast a large net of friends who better support them in every way of life. Many single people do this because they were lonely at one point while others chose this life because they enjoyed the extra time and independence arising from not being tied to a partner or family.

The research also found that in the case of single people, being more social gave them the confidence to feel they were not 'missing out' on anything. Developing meaningful relationships with people who have common interests, keeping in contact with family and friends, and pursuing pleasurable activities are crucial to alleviating loneliness when single.

Being single can be amazing, depending on how you view it. Apart from those reasons explained above, there are a few other reasons to remain single. You don't have to watch him and his friends play video games for hours. You don't have to worry about what he wants to eat, you only have to make a choice for yourself. You can go to the gym and check out that shirtless guy without feeling guilty. You get to have a crush on anybody you want. You will always be in control of the TV remote and you don't have to watch a show you hate. You can take all the time in the world to get ready without someone breathing down your neck. Bottom line is, being single comes with a lot of perks. It can be the best decision you've made in a long time.

Finally, remember: It is worse to be in a bad relationship than it is to be alone. According to a 2014 survey, people who have continuing tension in their relationships are less likely to appreciate the good moments in their lives. The worst part? The researchers point out that this tendency may also be a precursor to depression -- yikes!

CHAPTER SUMMARY

- One of the best decisions you can make for yourself is to remain single.
- There are many reasons to remain single which includes finding yourself.
- Saying single ladies are lonely is a myth that has been debunked. Go ahead and enjoy the perks of being single.

In the next chapter you will learn how to regain control over your life and stop playing by Society's rules as a woman.

CHAPTER FOUR: REGAINING CONTROL

It is important to learn how to stop playing by Society's rules for women. Society says you need a man by your side to feel complete and fulfilled. Society says if you can't keep a relationship, you have failed. Society says you should move heaven and earth to satisfy your man and not complain when he makes your life a living hell. Oh please! These are very unreasonable standards set for women, which are crap in my opinion. Society tries to muffle the person in us just to keep a relationship. I'm sure I speak for a lot of ladies when I say we are tired of Society's crappy rules and standards.

We have been conditioned to ask questions like: Will I ever find the man of my dreams? Will I ever get married? Will I ever have children? Will I live happily ever after with my Prince Charming? Of course, we all at some points asked these questions. I'm sure you've asked different variations of these questions. I remember when I was in my twenties, I thought that by the time I was thirty, I would be married or planning to get married. But, guess what? I am almost thirty and the only thing I care about right now is how to eat without gaining weight, have clear skin, have money, and travel around the world.

Don't get me wrong, there is nothing wrong with our initial dream. I am, in fact, proud of those women who have achieved it. But my point is this: if you still haven't achieved them, there is absolutely no reason to despair or feel bad or like you're a failure. Look, in life, there are no rules to follow. There is no standard timeline women have to follow. These "standards" and "rules" are societal crap. Life is not a shopping list that you must follow to the letter and mark off items as you - and everyone else - achieves each item. You only have one life to live and you owe it to yourself to live it to the fullest, pursuing your happiness. If your happiness depends on a man, I respect it (even though I don't think it should), only be careful to choose the man who makes you happy, who values you and respects you, otherwise you signed up for a lifetime of misery. I am going to be as real as possible because it's high time women put themselves first.

Holding on to the dream that Disney sold us since we were little, where every woman must be accompanied by her Prince Charming, is going to ultimately lead to us having miserable lives when we find out that fairy tales aren't real. There are people who are so completely obsessed with finding their Prince Charming that they forget to enjoy life as it comes and live in the moment. One of my friends suffers every time she sees an Instagram post about someone from her university getting married. The fact is that we all have different destinies and we aren't all cut out for the same thing. Just as there are those who are born to be doctors, surgeons, singers, writers, and models, there are those whose destinies are to be married, divorced, or single. While I am a strong believer of the ideology that we can rewrite our destinies, it doesn't mean you can't live and enjoy the present while trying to do that. You don't have to suffer through the process. Look, it is better to be single, enjoy the moment, and build yourself while waiting for a man who will complement you, love you and cherish you, than it is to settle for less and spend the rest of your life trying to fix your mistake.

Often, family pressure leads ladies to make bad decisions. We date someone who is bad for us simply so we don't have to go alone to family dinners. We settle with an abusive partner because our family members have been asking when we'll get married. Darling, you are the one in control of your life. It does not matter that your aunt keeps asking when you'll get married. You are the one who gets to choose when and with whom you will settle down. If you haven't found the right person yet, you just haven't. Screw them and their curiosity. If you end up with the wrong person due to the pressure, they sure as hell won't share in the pain. So, screw them.

Would you like to know another reason to get mad at societal pressure? Nobody ever asks, "How are you doing with that business project?" or "How far along are you in your career trajectory?" or even a general question, "Are you?" They will always ask about your relationship, your love life, which is sad because it shows that they believe that having a man next to you is what matters the most. But is it really the most important part of your life? The answer is simply no.

When you are single, people automatically think it's because you've had a failed relationship or you can't keep a man. Oh, this makes me laugh. It's simply ridiculous. Hello, I am single because I know that I am valuable, I respect myself, I am intelligent, I have a good physique, and I am independent. And until that man arrives who values who I am and treats me the way I should be treated, I will remain single. The day I find a man who is deserving of me, then I will start a relationship with that special someone. He will add value to my life, motivate me to want to be better, because I can always be better, he will take me on new adventures, to new and familiar places, and together we will make a powerful team and achieve all our goals. Until you find a man like this, remain single.

As I mentioned earlier, life is not a shopping list. There is no rule that says you are born, you grow, you marry, you reproduce, and you die. If you are already thirty and you are asked if you are married, if you have graduated, why you have not done these things, then you feel like you have failed. Oh, honey, life is not a list, and you don't owe it to anybody to meet their expectations, not even your parents. Nobody said that the norm is to finish college at 21, or get married at 24. There is no standard timeline for living. You have to draw out your own timeline, on your terms, putting only your happiness into consideration. When I say only, I mean only. You don't have to put Society's opinion into consideration. It is your life and nobody, absolutely nobody, gets to decide how you live it.

Each stage of your life should be lived to the fullest. You only have one life to live and you must live it to the point where you can boldly say, "If I die tomorrow I will be proud of myself because I lived life to the fullest and I have no regrets." As women, we seem to have a lower chance of enjoying life because we think we have a particular order we have to follow in living our lives. We are born, we should go to school, we should have a career, but nothing too big or we might scare away men, we should find a man to settle down with even if that's not what we want, we should give birth to children and then append the rest of our lives raising them. Look, if this is what you want, then by all means, go ahead as long as it makes you happy. But if this doesn't sit well with you, then girl, build that life you want, Society be damned.

There are some mind-sets we need to change and adopt new ones if we are to break free from Society's hold.

THROW AWAY THE STEREOTYPES

Men are commonly described as having characteristics such as competence, achievement-orientation, tendency to take control, autonomy and rationality, whereas women are described as having characteristics associated with empathy for others, habits of association, deference, and emotional sensitivity. Such traits are not only described as being distinct for each gender, they appear to be oppositional: on average, people agree that men should not be too warm and women should not be too dominant. Research has been comprehensive on these generalizations, and demonstrates that they are common depictions across history, time, and cultures. These stereotypes tend to dictate how women should live their lives. The stereotype says that the only thing women desire is to be someone's partner. When you want to be single, therefore, you feel like there is something wrong with you.

Rest assured that being single at any point of your life would not force you to live like a nun. The elements that make up a full emotional life are intimacy, friendship, passion, and romance, and all of these elements are available to the unmarried. Our impediment is that we were programmed to demean or be afraid of the single life. Fairy tales inform us of lonely people living alone as twisted and sad. Remember the cliché of the single woman: a woman living alone whose only company is her cats. We continue to condemn these clichés and stereotypes, since we believe that someone who longs to live alone would become eccentric and that eccentricity is viewed as negative. I am inclined to equate single life with eccentricity and accept it as an expression of the independence that people who live alone enjoy by themselves. So let's celebrate eccentricity, identifying it as what it is — individuality in the adventure of enjoying one's own company. Cheers for free choice! It is one of the main advantages of living alone, as opposed to making compromises with a soul mate, on a non-soul mate.

Ladies should aim to be eccentric. We should no longer conform to the norms and stereotypes of the past that try to keep us bound. If we are ever going to be truly free, we need to discard societal stereotypes and relationship stereotypes. Not only would we be breaking free from relationship stereotypes, we will be kicking career stereotypes to the curb. The only way to achieve this is to renew our mind-sets.

Let's start with workplace stereotypes. Part of gaining control of your life includes career success. Women will be doing three things to improve their mind-set and in turn break free from stereotypes in the workplace: Learn, Step Up, Speak Out.

LEARNING: STRENGTH IN KNOWLEDGE

Have you ever felt like your repair shop has ripped you off? A study found that auto-repair shops change their price quotes according to how knowledgeable callers seem to be about costs associated with their vehicle. If callers stated they had no idea what the cost of the repair would be (usually women), they would be given a higher price than those who did know the price (usually men). This example illustrates how a single piece of information can help reduce some gender-related discrimination and may also begin a chain reaction that changes the perceptions of car mechanics towards women. Interestingly, the study also showed that a woman is more likely to get a lower price from the repair shop if she asks; educated women eventually obtained an advantage over men. If you want to break stereotypes in Society and in the workplace, you need to learn more. Put yourself on the same playing field as a man. When you are as knowledgeable as any man, you cannot be held down by stereotypes.

STEP INTO MALE-DOMINATED AREAS

Until people realize that stereotypes are negative and systemic, they won't vanish. If women don't step up and get in Society's face, things won't change. As a woman who aims to demolish stereotypes and do whatever the hell she wants, you will need to put yourself in areas and situations that are dominated by men and demand what you want with boldness. You have the right to do whatever you want as a woman without anybody telling you that you can't because your vision is meant for a man or can only be accomplished by a man. The next time someone tries to undermine you or your goals because you are a woman, get in his face, demand what you want and tell him to stop embarrassing himself.

PREPARE TO REACT AND SPEAK OUT

Women should expect comments which are offensive or discriminatory and plan to respond accordingly. When people try to make you act according to a stereotype, you have to put them back in their place and stand your ground. When people ask questions or make remarks that are derogatory, do not take it lying down. Although these questions or remarks have in the past been appropriate, it is our job today to ensure that they are no longer acceptable. Those perpetuating perceptions of gender will bear the implications of such behaviour. A recent example is the apology of Martin Solveig at the Ballon d'Or ceremony after he made a sexist remark. We have to recognize our own prejudices and retrain our brains to conquer them. Life may not be equal but there is something we can do about it.

Now, to stereotypes in relationships. Society makes us feel like we need a man to be complete, as though our highest achievement in life is to be somebody's wife or girl-friend. Many women spend their time searching for a partner because they want to fit into Society's image of a proper woman. Sometimes, I want to scream and tell them that they don't need a man to complete them.

You don't have to buy into the narrative of "he completes me," which seems to be a common phrase. You don't have to believe you have to be with a guy so you can feel happy in your life. You have to stop believing you have to be in a rela-tionship to really have a life worth living. Concentrate on building your own life that you can be proud of. Live your own life to the fullest – regardless of whether or not your life is one with romantic relationships in it. You don't have to wait before the special person comes into your life before you begin to understand how unique your life is already. You're the one who calls the shots. You are your own lifelong boss. You're the one who has the power to determine how your life will turn out. You don't need a guy to make you feel vali-dated. You don't need to make a guy to add meaning to your precious life. You should make the most of your life by fulfilling your dreams and making time for your passions. You need to be the one who meets your own needs. You have to be the one who sustains your own reality. Look, you cannot afford to rely on anyone to give you a sense of fulfil-ment; humans are very fickle and unreliable. You don't need to have a guy in your life to feel like you can overcome any obstacles that the universe may send your way. You are a badass already and you don't need a man to make you feel like one. You must be able to adapt on your own and you must trust in your ability to navigate through the trials this life may bring.

The fact that you're not in a romantic relationship doesn't mean you have no relationships that need to be nurtured. Those bonds that you share with your friends and family need to be nourished. You have more opportunities to show love to someone than when you are in a romantic relationship. You must also be able to give and express love to those people who love you, like your friends and family. I won't deny the fact that a romantic relationship would be a different kind of affection and attention, but the fact that you're not in one doesn't mean you're not wanted. You are always loved by people who deserve your affection and attention just as much as a partner would. Offer your time to these people in your life and show them their worth to you. You need those connections that you have with them to be able to build your strong, loving foundations. If you continually put yourself in a place with loving relationships with friends and family, you're not going to feel the stresses of trying to find a guy to be with.

You have to understand that being in a relationship should be a matter of choice and not because you feel the pressure to be in one or because Society says it's the right thing to do at a particular age, whatever that particular happens to be. Yes, you can make it a personal destination to eventually be in a relationship with someone you love. But that goal shouldn't be your only goal. That's not going to be what distinguishes you or defines you. You shouldn't have your fulfilment tied to falling in love with someone else. You have to be able to find fulfillment for yourself, in yourself, and it must be something that you don't rely on someone else for. You should set your own goals and be sure that they're not tied to someone because people can be grossly unreliable.

One moment they're there and the next they aren't. You're destined to be so much more than someone's girlfriend or wife. You have to really know what your worth is. You must realize that you are indeed as amazing as amazing gets and you don't need a boyfriend to prove that to you.

Will it be great to be in a relationship with someone you love? Absolutely. Yet, you shouldn't take that to mean you're incapable of living a wonderful life when you're single. You can do so many amazing things all by yourself. You are capable of spectacular feats without relying on someone else. You are indeed deserving of your own excellence. Many people are making the mistake of believing that happiness is not a choice. It actually is. You can either let your circumstances pin you down or you can choose to rise above them and find your own peace in this universe. Sure, you might not presently have a relationship. That doesn't mean, however, that there aren't a million other things you should be happy with in this life. There'll always be a reason to be happy. You only need to look around to see. There'll always be a cause to be grateful and you have to realize that as early as now. You need to find peace inside yourself and the world you already live in.

I cannot emphasize enough that you don't need a man or a relationship to feel complete and fulfilled. People can't be trusted with something like that. It's too much power for anything human. If you need a man to make you happy, complete, and fulfilled, what about the day he suddenly decides that he no longer wants to be with you? Your world is going to come crumbling down and you will blame the guy. No, it's going to be your fault because your world shouldn't depend on him in the first place.

All I'm saying is that you are an incredible someone before you become someone's girlfriend. Let the person that you are be all shades of amazing on her own, without a man.

I understand that this isn't the way that Society wants us to think but we are - right now! - dumping every stereotype in the refuse bin. We are breaking the hold Society has had over our minds. We are no longer going to think our ultimate goal as women is to be married. We are taking back our lives and we are going to live to the fullest.

Never again are we going to conform to stereotypes.

Never again are we going to judge our worth based solely on a relationship.

Never again are we going to get into relationships that aren't necessarily good for us because we want to feel like we are worthy of love and that this is the only way we think or have been told that we can feel that worth.

We now know that even without a man, we are worthy of love.

We now know that we are amazing badass women.

We now know that our ultimate goal is to live our lives to the fullest on our own terms.

We are now free from Society's stereotypes.

And screw whoever thinks we are aiming too high: we can do whatever the hell we desire.

GO BACK TO THE DRAWING BOARD AND DRAW A REVISED PLAN FOR YOUR LIFE

Now that we know that we are not bound by any stereotype, it is time to plan that life that you've always wanted to live.

As single women in a search of a relationship, marriage or a family of our own, we are likely to inhibit our aspirations and ambitions, sometimes consciously, sometimes unknowingly. Do you agree with this or can you relate with it? Your answer may be a yes, may be a no. Before you answer, take a few moments to look back on your life and all the things you'd hoped to do. Where are you from where you started? How did your plans change or evolve?

Ask yourself if you stalled on any of those dreams because you wanted to do them when you were married or in a relationship? Ask yourself what the problem actually is: why are you still waiting? Do you feel like if you're busy chasing your ambitions and dreams, you're not going to have time to socialize or be noticed by people, namely your potential partner? We feel like if we pursue our dreams and end up succeeding, we will frighten off the potential men, since, according to the stereotype, they cannot handle our success or might feel emasculated. We will also speculate that dwelling on achieving these dreams and goals would also lead people to believe that we don't want to marry.

There's always that part of us which isn't sure of our intent and the things we should do. We may think the most important thing we could ever do as women is to get married and have kids. You're probably wondering where this all leads so here's the bottom line: I would like to challenge that you do more. Live the life God gave you, confidently and without reservation. If he asked you not to wait another second, then start now! He's already given everything that you need. Pursuing and realizing this vision, possibly realizing more than what you could have ever imagined, would not deter you from getting married if this is what you really want. No, living your life unapologetically provides the groundwork for you to meet the right guy to marry.

Think about it, if you avoided doing those things before you got married so that you don't scare the guy, why do you think things are going to be alright when you're married or in a relationship? A man who hates your potential, your goals, and your ambition is unlikely to start loving them when you're married. You will find out that because of his insecurities and fears, you will always be living in the shadows unable to bloom. Given his feelings about your dreams and how they define you as who you really are, if you do decide to follow these dreams, this might lead to a break-down of the relationship or marriage. Sounds grim but it's so real and I've heard and seen it in relationships.

Do yourself a favor and live life the way you want and do not apologize for it. If you want to pursue a career, do it. If you want to go back to school, do it. Live life on your terms. It is time to plan your life the way you want to see it, show up for it, and succeed in it.

HAVE A DEEP DESIRE TO LIVE ANOTHER LIFE AND HAVE A REASON TO PURSUE IT

What's going on in your life that you're unhappy about? What drives you now to want your life changed? Is there anything missing, something that you are looking for? If you have a considerable level of constructive dissatisfaction, this will prompt you to make a change. If your wish is strong enough, you'll find a way to make your dreams become your reality. That desire gives you your big reason that keeps you pushing forward against any obstacles that might come up and threaten to derail your plan. Journaling about your dissatisfaction, what you want to create instead, and why that is important to you, is a good idea. Write out what you are not satisfied with about your life. Write out the things you want to do with your life and why you want to do them. This way, when you face obstacles, you can go back to your journal and find some motivation.

FIND YOUR PASSION

I've never met someone who'd dreamed of working 40-60 hours a week to make someone else wealthy. It is possible that finding your passion will lead you to becoming an entrepreneur, but it may also lead to creating a charitable organization. You have a purpose in life and a passion for something which is yours and yours alone. No one else has the same mix of passion and intent you have. If you were a belly dancing teacher with a busload of belly dancing teachers and all of you moved to Bali together, you would still have a different, unique vision for your dream life. There are no two people who express their passion for a particular thing in exactly the same way. Depending on the context of your life experiences, the sense you made out of those experiences and the lessons you learned from them, you would be a belly dancing teacher teaching belly dancing a little differently from all the other teachers. Take some time to ponder what you value, what excites you, what you love to do. Write it all out, so that you can see it before you. Sometimes you have to write things down for them to start becoming real to you. You can have a passion you want to pursue, but until you write it down where you can see it, it doesn't have the opportunity to become real.

WORK OUT A PLAN

Now that you know why and where you want to make a change, what you want that change to be, and what passion in your dream life you will be fulfilling, it's time to create your plan. Making a plan might look like setting targets and dividing those targets into actionable steps. It may also be that you want to go deeper and create a reality for your life from a dream that involves peeling the layers away to find your own authentic self and dissecting all those masks wherever you are. It is crucial to have a clear written plan. The first step is then to make this first move. If you've properly planned your strategy, you can take some simple steps right now that will get you on the road to living the life of your dreams. The little steps need to give the forward momentum to get going, without being so large they scare you into inaction. If you are freezing instead of going forward, take the step down a notch and try. Better to make one step into two or four steps than to struggle with one huge step that stops you from living your dream.

WHEN YOU ASK YOURSELF, "What is my dream in life?" I hope you don't start your answer with a dollar sign. Money does not buy good fortune, happiness or fulfilment. That is an actual reality. Money frustrates and disappoints more people than anything else. You're starting to make the big bucks, you're buying a big house, a more expensive car, getting all the toys and joining all the right clubs to tell the world you made it. Money never will make you a better person. Money will never make you happy. It can bring you joy and freedom, but your life still needs substance. If your life doesn't have any meaning, you'll be a very unhappy person and you definitely won't be living your dream life.

You don't want to build a cash trap where you're on a treadmill to keep making more and more to give the high to yourself. When you don't have a clear strategy, your hard-earned money might turn into negative acquisitions, like alcohol or drugs. I'm sure that adding these negative things to your life is not part of what you imagined when you wrote out your dreams. I'm asking now because nobody can answer the question except you, as you might have suspected. These scenarios are not anything that you should be answering from the top of your head since you've done everything you can to build a solid plan.

Once you consider a reason bigger than yourself, the burning desire turns into a roaring fire. Your passion is pushing you and all of the pieces begin to fall into place. You'll find the people and processes, the things you didn't have any idea how to do or where to find, will show up to help and guide you.

HOW DO I START LIVING MY LIFE ON MY OWN?

The first step toward living your own life is to make a decision that you will do exactly that: make your own decisions. Things start shifting when you draw a line in the sand that lets everyone in your life know you're taking over and you're going to be in charge right now. Avoid telling someone what they think they should be doing. They haven't even worked their own life out, so they definitely shouldn't be in charge of yours. So few people take the time to develop their lives intentionally by developing a dream for their future and a strategy to make it a reality. If you take the time and do the work right now you can create your dream life and start living it intentionally. You can take total control of your life and flourish even when you don't have a romantic relationship.

I need you to always remember that you don't need a man to complete you. You are fabulous on your own and you can live the life of your dreams without a man. If you eventually decide to be in a romantic relationship with a man, he will be lucky to have you.

CHAPTER SUMMARY

- To take back control of your life, you have to defy stereotypes.
- To defy stereotypes, you need to keep learning.

- Make sure to step into male-dominated areas and speak up with boldness.
- Prepare to react whenever anybody tries to shove stupid stereotypes down your throat.

IN THE NEXT chapter you will learn that you are in charge of your relationship life.

CHAPTER FIVE: NOW, YOU'RE IN CONTROL

O ften, I want to pull women aside and tell them, "You are in control of your relationship life." When it comes to a relationship between a man and a woman, the woman should call the shots, not the other way round. Women have given up the power we are supposed to have in our relationships. You are in control of who you let into your life. You are in control of who you fall for. You are in control of how a man treats you. Yes, these are facts.

Sadly, we women do not realize this. Instead, we continually let ourselves be treated like crap, we set aside our dreams and aspirations for men, and we put them first. It's just plain wrong. You should come first and not a man. Think about it: why do men today not want a serious relationship? Part of it is because they do not have the time, because they are focused on their professional development and they see marrying as secondary to their aspirations. When men already have a full life and want to transcend, then they decide to put efforts into relationships. When they see something as temporary or not necessary, they do not put in enough effort into making that something a success. I think we should take a page from men's books and start treating ourselves better. A man would never give up on a dream, goal or career to be with a woman. He would never allow himself to be disrespected in a relationship because he wants to be in that relationship. Men put themselves first, and if the relationship is not convenient for them, they break it off. Women need to start acting like this in order to have happy lives and relationships. Let's look at an example of a woman who has a successful life and is in a relationship with a successful man who is worth her time. What these two people in this relationship have in common is that they are both busy, they are both seeking to meet their goals, they both have emotional independence, and between the two, they help each other while enjoying their company. These two won't have petty issues, nobody feels insecure, nobody suspects unfaithfulness because both parties are busy and, presumably, trust each other. This is how it should be.

When you have something important going on in your life, and then you decide to let a man into your life who doesn't have anything going on for him, you have signed up for a miserable relationship because he is going to feel threatened by you. In situations like this, the guy starts asking her to give up her career or ambition for him to calm his insecurities. This is the last thing you want to do as a woman: give up the life you're working on for a man. If the tables were turned, would he do the same for you? Let me answer that: No.

There are certain guardrails you can put in place so you are always in control of your relationship life.

NEVER SETTLE FOR SOMETHING LESS

I have met many women who settled for guys who aren't what they want simply because they want to be in a relationship. It's sad when women settle for less because they think they can't do better.

I'll say it for as long as it takes you to understand: you are fabulous and you deserve an equally fabulous man. You shouldn't settle for less. It's better to be single than to be in a relationship with a man you don't want.

If you are currently in a relationship with a guy you don't love or want, now is the perfect time to leave the relationship. You can't remain in an unhappy relationship because you think that any relationship is better than none. You're way more valuable than that. Let your partner know you are confident, and know what you deserve. When one partner is able to get away with something then the control of the other is lost. It is important to stand up and hold your ground. When something doesn't fit the way you want, don't be afraid to walk away, either. Show that your emotions and your choices are in your control.

RESPECT, DEFEND YOURSELF

You have to know that his bad or inappropriate conduct towards you can't be tolerated anymore and needs to stop now. Remember, he won't change until you start treating yourself better. He treats you the way you treat yourself. If you don't respect yourself, he won't either. If you are in a relationship with someone who doesn't respect you, you need to make the change and see to it that you get the respect you deserve. You can only boost your emotional connection with a person if you have self-respect and trust. You should be able to claim, "I can live on my own and I do not need a boyfriend." If your boyfriend realizes that you don't need him, he'll come to you because people always want something they can't have. If you don't have respect for yourself, no one else will have respect for you. Support is important in relationships so show your partner that you support yourself. Take care of how you are thinking about yourself, how you are dealing with power and how you are seeing your character. Your partner will echo and reflect this respect back to you.

DON'T ALWAYS BE AVAILABLE

No matter what you do, don't wait for your boyfriend to make your evening plans with you because you are hoping or assuming he will ask you out. If you have plans, then go ahead with them. He should want to hang out with you without a doubt. Most importantly, you won't have to focus too much on your budding relationship if you keep busy yourself. You are not going to overthink the messages you send him and you'll reply to his texts in an appropriate time frame, waiting very conscientiously for his answer. We all do it but it's sort of sad.

Whether it's a budding relationship or a long term relationship, you shouldn't always be available. He needs to know that if he wants you to be available, he should tell you beforehand. It typically means not always making yourself available to him, not because you choose not to be available, but because you have your own wonderful life full of friends and family who you also want to spend with.

Make sure your partner knows you have a life outside the relationship without playing games. That's particularly essential in the beginning because they shouldn't think you're too vulnerable. Show them that you love yourself, that without them you will complete yourself and that your relationship with them adds to the wonderful life that you already have. It should help you find out how you can be in control in a relationship. This puts you in control of the relationship. Remember: A man is a wonderful addition to your life as a full human, not the missing piece of your life that you cannot live without. You should love yourself and be complete and happy, with or without a man.

WORK ON YOUR EMOTIONS

You can only respect yourself when you have a balanced attitude. Your relationship is going to follow suit, and be rock-solid if you're both coming into it with a balanced attitude. The secret is mental and emotional intelligence. Emotional intelligence sees to it that you are always in charge of your emotions and this is very important in any relationship. Emotional intelligence will help you keep your emotions in check so you don't make decisions based on your emotions. In addition, if you want him to respect you, you must present him with someone to respect. You can't let your emotions be all over the place and expect him to respect you. You need to work on your emotions so that while starting a new relationship, you can control your relationship and with maturity and grace.

HAVE BOUNDARIES

Each person has their own set of rules and boundaries for themself that they're at ease with. You're going to have limits in your relationship and it's important that you keep them. For you, there are some issues that can cross the line and you need to be able to draw the line firmly and express that clearly. For you to be in control of your relationship, you need to set boundaries. Setting boundaries applies to platonic relationships, too. Whether you are in an already existing relationship or a budding one, there have to be boundaries for him to respect you. Boundaries help you to be in control of the relationships in your life. You get to put a guy in check when he's overstepping. If you don't have boundaries, there is no way of doing this. You probably have your own set of rules that fall within your comfort zone, so when you are in a relationship, it's important to keep some of those. If you have no boundaries and are feeling the need for more power, seek to set those boundaries so you're comfortable moving forward. Know your boundaries and talk to your partner clearly about them. Make sure your partner understands that it does not mean no and affirm your decision with truthful words of support. Boundaries show what we support and disagree with, especially in areas that cause tension. Give straightforward yes-or-no responses with supporting statements validating your decisions or behaviors.

STICK TO YOUR WORDS

Saying something and doing the opposite is one way to lose someone's respect very quickly. What you do speaks louder than what you say — especially in relationships. Therefore, if you warn your friend that something they may do will have certain consequences and you don't follow through, he or she will not take you seriously the next time they cross that boundary. Even when you make a small commitment to your partner, you have to keep that promise. Say what you mean and mean what you say. You can't take charge of your relationship if you don't follow through with your words. There are many ways for you to be in control of a relationship. If you want your partner to take it more seriously and gain a little more control in a particular area, then make sure your words and your actions match in the follow-through. If you act in accordance with your comments, your partner will feel the difference, and will respect you more. Also, if you are having a conflict with your partner, you want to make sure to follow through and act on the resolutions you both come up with together. If you think there are going to be any consequences, then make sure you stick to your decisions. If you always give in or go against your word, your partner won't take you seriously. It works the same way when keeping promises: make sure that you are truthful, and do as you say you will.

DON'T WASTE YOUR TIME ON SOMEONE WHO'S PLAYING GAMES

An adult partnership is one where the authority is controlled and if you want to play games then you mess with the balance of power. You don't want to date someone who likes to play and is good at such games, since they also take care of you. Gain leverage over childish games in your relationship by demonstrating you don't need to get into a power struggle. You really do not want to be in a relationship where the guy plays games with you. If he doesn't get serious, you need to show him you're not one to be played with by dumping him. As someone who is self-confident, you would never allow such games to be played: walk away, as you should.

CHAPTER SUMMARY

- The most important thing in this chapter is for you to know that the power in a relationship resides with you.
- You are in control of who you allow into your life.
- You are in control of who you fall for.

- You are in control of how a man treats you. Don't give that power away.

IN THE NEXT chapter you will learn how to know if a guy is interested in you or not, as well as all the excuses guys give when they are not into you.

CHAPTER SIX: A MASTER OF THE GAME

How do you know if a guy is really into you or if you should delete his number and move on? We are going to go through some of the excuses that guys give and how to know if he's not into you.

There's one question that you never want to say out loud, that runs through your head incessantly when dating – "Is he really that in me?" This age-old problem still appears to be a mystery today, but why? After all, it should surely be easy to notice if a guy has taken a serious fancy to your cute self. Why do the signals become so difficult to decipher? Why can't he come right out and say that he's into you? Is he pretending so he can take you to bed and that's it? The good news is that actions speak louder than words. When it comes down to it, his actions would prove his intentions if he is really interested in you for more than just a fling. Game players, while confident that they can woo you with words, will usually not back those words up with sincere effort. How can you tell if he is being truthful? If you think the guy you've met and are interested in could be a player, you don't have to take his word for it or take him at face value - you need to take note of his actions. Doing so also helps you to decipher intentions, unless your guy is willing to express his feelings with words and that takes time to build up that trust.

Here are few ways to know if he's really into you.

HE WILL PROACTIVELY CALL AND TEXT YOU

There is nothing worse than giving your number to a guy and expectantly waiting for a text which never comes. Then, you do hear from him at 2:00 am on a Saturday morning two weeks later. While you can think of a million reasons for why he hasn't made an attempt before this, such behavior is generally a sure-fire indication that he's not in you. On the other hand, a man who is interested in you truly thinks about you. He'll reach out to say hello, to see how your day is going, or to share something funny and make you laugh. More than likely, he would find any excuse to call to hear your voice or say how much he enjoyed your date. If he's into you, he contacts you simply because you are on his mind: he can't help it and he needs to make sure he's on yours, too. When you're with a guy who sends you a good morning text to see when you wake up without him, it's possible that he's excited about you and your new relationship. Starting and finishing the day with you on his mind means you are the diversion that will make him happy whether he's at home during the night or during the day when he's at work. When the time comes, within the probability of sex, he is curious and not interested in rushing.

HE INCLUDES YOU IN HIS LIFE

If a guy showers you with presents and lavishes attention on you but doesn't involve you in his life, chances are that he isn't really in you. He would tell his friends about the fantastic girl he's met when he's genuinely interested, he'll mention you to work mates and maybe even to his family. You will obviously encounter people in his life as time goes by, and you will involve each other in your social lives. It's pretty hard to stay quiet though, even initially, when you really like somebody. So, if he feels your relationship is going anywhere, if he mentions you to anyone in his inner circle, you'll soon find out. Although the talk does not involve ring shopping, he's a guy who sees you by his side whenever he mentions stuff he wants to do in the future, such as a weekend away, going with him to a concert for which he has tickets or sharing relationship goals. It's really easy to pick it up from your conversations if he sees you in his future. When a guy isn't into you, he will let it slip sooner or later when he talks about his future plans and you're not in them.

HE WILL ARRANGE TO SEE YOU

Although it is true that guys also feel anxious about potentially being rejected, a man who is into you would totally want to see you, and would proactively make plans to do so -- for more than a late night booty call. He will invite you out for dinner, ask if you want to have a coffee before work, take you to the beach for a swim, something where you're going to spend time together. You see, he's being compelled to act. He wants to do something that's perfect for you. It is because you occupy a fair amount of his space in his thoughts and it makes him happy every time you pop into his brain. If a man dates several women, he will see one on Friday and another on Saturday to see who he will finally place higher on his dating totem pole. If he wants to see you several days in a row over a long period of time, including both weekend nights, it's a sign you're probably his one-and-only.

THE BODY LANGUAGE IS GOING TO TELL YOU

Body language speaks volumes if you can't count on words. Eye contact is the big one because none of us can help but look into a person's eyes that we are attracted to seriously. He will also look to your eyes and back to your lips, because kissing you will never be far from his mind.

He's going to angle his pelvis towards you when you're standing together and when you're sitting down he's going to lean in close to talk. Physical touch is a dead giveaway, particularly if he tucks your hair behind your ear, directs you gently to the door, or 'accidentally' brushes your arm regularly. It's true that the same signals mean he wants you in his bed, but that's not the only thing he wants to do with you when combined with other signs. We prefer to lean toward people we want without knowing it and we lean away from those we do not like. When you talk to that man, watch if he turns his body towards you or away from you. You can also see if his feet are pointing towards you, which could be another indication he is interested in. You can tell a lot from someone's body signals.

HE LISTENS TO YOU AND UNDERSTANDS WHAT YOU ARE SAYING TO HIM

When a man really likes you, his deep curiosity lights up and he will be ready to listen to what you have to say. He will ask questions and express his willingness to learn about what you think, feel, don't like and do in the world in general. He wants to see the woman underneath the physical, beyond the attraction. You're going to know the extent of his interest because he will remember things you tell him. Whether it's buying your favorite candy, wishing you luck for an important meeting that you discussed last week, or playing a song that you love dancing to, his acts will prove his attraction and concern.

HE GETS KIND OF NERVOUS AROUND YOU

Sometimes, when a guy likes you, he can get a little bashful. If you notice that a guy blushes, stammers, or becomes quiet when you come around, he might have a crush on you even though he might be naturally shy. Try to give him a little smile or a touch on the arm to reassure him if you notice a guy doing this if you like him, too! It can help in making him feel at ease.

While you get butterflies whenever you see your boyfriend, you have to know he may get nervous about you, too. All that you feel, he's probably feeling, too. He might act nervous if he likes you, then. Various people interpret nervousness in various ways. He could talk really quickly and not pause for a breath or let you say something. He may stutter. He might have shaky hands. He might even be telling bad jokes. Realize that what you could assume to be self-centeredness — like him talking overtop of you or not answering you questions — may be a case of nerves, so think twice before you write it off as his not being interested. Think about what you do when you get nervous around a guy you like. Check for signals like those, so that you know he feels the same.

HE MIGHT BE A BIT TACTILE

Boys like to interact. Some do so in a way that gets them slapped. That's not the type of touch you're looking for. You are instead looking for little innocent touches like on your arm or shoulder. A man that likes you finds excuses to touch you. He might touch your arm while he's talking or he might help you to adjust your clothes so he can touch you. Little innocent touches. He shows he's into you because boys generally get touchy when they like a girl. If a guy is always ready with a hug or he often touches you on your arm or shoulder, he's showing that he likes you without actually saying so by being physically close to you. He may, however, be a touchy-feely guy, if he is behaving around other people like that. He definitely has a crush if you're the only one he behaves like this with. When a guy makes you feel awkward by touching or pushing past you, tell him firmly to stop and move away from him. Don't worry about his feelings being hurt. If he's a good guy, he's going to apologize and will not repeat it again. If it does go on, stay away from him.

We've looked at different signs that show a guy is into you. How do you know, then, if a guy isn't into you?

HE'S LETTING YOU TAKE ALL THE BIG STEPS ALONE

When a guy leaves you to take any big step, he's not into you. When a guy likes you, he won't let you be the one to arrange all the dates, sleepovers and all. When you notice that you are the only one making the effort in the relationship, then he is definitely not into you. When you are the one pushing for things to happen and offering everything on a platter of gold, you both are going nowhere because he won't appreciate everything you do. Guys don't appreciate what they didn't have to work for.

I remember when one of my best friends was dating this guy. Everything was fine, she had the situation under control, when suddenly, in less than four months she had moved to live at his house and she took all her things. He lived with his family, his life remained unchanged, he was comfortable with his house, his space, his family and now a bonus: his girl-friend. What more could he ask for? She, on the other hand, was very uncomfortable with not having her space with her boyfriend. She did not feel comfortable going to the kitchen, cooking, getting up late on her days off for fear that her boyfriend's mother would think she was lazy. A couple of months passed and guess what? Don't get your hopes up. He didn't ask her to marry or move into a new apartment with him. Instead, she had to find a new apartment to move into because the routine of this life with her boyfriend became a nightmare. She was at a worse point than she was before going to live with him. She considered different options and felt that she should offer him a place at her apartment, in the hope of starting that beautiful story that she had in mind with him. Guess what? He did not accept her offer and to this day he lives with his family.

The reason why this guy didn't appreciate her moving in is because he got the benefits of the relationship handed to him on a gold platter without having to compromise. He didn't have to beg her to move in, he didn't have to marry her, nothing. She was the only one taking steps, taking the risks, in the relationship and the guy was obviously not into her.

The reality is that when everything is handed to them on a golden platter, men do not want to make an effort. It is normal: the same thing happens to us. Think about that man, the one we all have had a relationship with at some point: he's a good person, he's attractive, he's available 24 hours a day, 7 days a week for you. Did you like him? No. He could be an option, but why didn't you like him? Because he was available. It was easy and effortless; it does not create a challenge. You weren't interested in him because you didn't have to do anything to win him, he would come to you. Same for guys. If he's leaving everything up to you to do and you keep taking the steps and the risks, then he doesn't really like you.

HE DOESN'T ASK ABOUT YOU AND YOUR LIFE

When a man shows no interest or curiosity in finding out who you are, then this is not a positive indication that he likes you. Normally, we can't get enough when we like someone. We want to know every single story, every single detail. We pay keen attention when they talk about their lives and we ask follow up questions. We look for similarities that we can relate to and differences we can grow with because we want to know everything there is to know about them. The takeaway here is if a guy shows no interest in your life, your hobbies, what you enjoy, and so on, he's not really all that interested in you.

He's not concerned about your job and never asks about your day. You let it go because, after not seeing each other for a day or more, it is usually good to chat and catch up about other things. This can become a bit of a concern if he never asks how your day was. Is he aware of what you're doing for work? Is he mindful of where you're headed every day? Does he seem to be in tune with the way you look when you come home from work? Does he ever wonder why you look down or upset or really happy about something that happened when he wasn't there? Failure to inquire about your day shows he doesn't care, and it isn't something to look past. After time, that could be a strong indication for you that he's not the right one for you.

HE PUTS YOU DOWN AND MAKES YOU FEEL LIKE CRAP

When he makes you feel bad about yourself with subtle, backhanded comments, he lowers your self-esteem. Then it's a simple indication that you're actually not benefiting from the relationship and he's not really loving you. Being on the receiving end of an offensive attack is never fun. You may be telling yourself to ignore the demeaning remarks, but some of it may eventually stay with you, and you're worried that something is very "wrong." Anyone who makes you feel bad about yourself, even though it may not be deliberate, probably doesn't like you to begin with. Someone who cares about you will never intentionally make you feel bad about yourself and when they do so mistakenly, they immediately apologize.

This is one of the biggest signs of a toxic relationship and it seems like it would be pretty black and white, but often you don't even realize all the ways he puts you down because it can be done in sneaky ways that aren't flat-out criticisms. Relationships represent an opportunity for huge personal growth. Our less-than-stellar qualities are sometimes brought to the surface and they need to be addressed. There is, however, a huge difference between a partner who can lovingly point out your flaws in a way that encourages you to grow and a partner who points out your shortcomings from a place of contempt. If it was a healthy relationship, he will accept you for who you are. He's going to love the good and accept the bad because we're all human, we're all flawed, and bad qualities come along with being human. Anyone who expects perfection in a partner paves the way for a lifetime of disappointment. You'll want to improve when you're in a healthy relationship because you truly want to be your best self — for your sake, for your partner's sake, and for the sake of the relationship. In a healthy relationship, you will feel loved and accepted for who you are, and both you and he will understand that it takes time to change, so from time to time you will not feel bad about succumbing to some of your negative qualities. You're never going to feel accepted in a toxic relationship, your partner's going to have little tolerance for your negative qualities, and he will continue to shame you and belittle you for them.

HE DOESN'T CALL YOU AND THEN HE MAKES EXCUSES

He's busy at work. He's tired. He's got a million things going on. His whole world is burning down. There are more excuses for why he doesn't call you than there are phone calls.

When he likes you, it doesn't matter how busy he is. He's going to take at least 30 of the 86,400 seconds in a day to contact you, even if it's only to send a quick email. A guy who spends more time sending the excuses out early on is always a bad omen. At the beginning of a relationship there is no continuity or certitude. For all that he knows, you've got a line of guys waiting on you for their turn. When he is into you, he's not going to risk any other guy snatching you up while working on a job because he was "too busy."

A worse sign is when he says he will call but he ends up not calling. When a guy says he's going to call you tomorrow and then he doesn't call until two or three days later, means you're not a priority for him. You want to go out again with him? Fine, whatever. You start dating a different guy? Whatever, he doesn't care. When a man is into you, he is going to call when he says he's going to. Looking back at my own lengthy experience of dating, the guys who were calling when they said they would are the ones who were genuine and very into me. The relationships with the guys who made me sweat it out and didn't follow through with reliable communication never lasted longer than three dates. If a man likes you, he is going to bring his A-game. People are inherently competitive. No guy would let some other dude grab a girl he wants. If he says he will call after a date and he ends up not calling, dump his sorry ass. He's not serious.

It's honestly not that difficult to tell whether a guy is into you or not. Most times, we want to hope for the best and ignore the potentially negative signs in front of us. This is why a lot of us end up heartbroken. If you have to wonder if a guy is into you or not, chances are that he's not. Take mixed signals as a no. Guys always make it obvious when they are into you and you never really have to wonder. If he makes you doubt him, he's most probably not into you or he has an ulterior motive.

Never ignore a red flag. No matter how amazing this guy is and how desperately you want the relationship to work, if there are red flags, they're a sign of danger you can't ignore. You need to get out before things get worse. Red flags aren't hard to recognize. We ignore them, and ignore our intuition, hoping the red flag isn't what we think it is. We hope it'll go away or improve by ignoring it. It doesn't work that way.

Usually we ignore red flags because we are scared that they tell the real, painful story. We may ask our partners questions about their actions and receive the answers that we want to hear. Even if those answers aren't what we want them to be, we leave them alone. We do not want to learn the facts. If we found out the truth, we'd have to change something — our entire life, the place we live, our finances, maybe even ourselves. That can be too exhausting to think about. Even if we're sure it's happening, we don't want our partner to say the truth because of what that would mean for us, our families and our lives. We don't want to see their bad habits or bad behavior because we might actually have to walk out of the relationship.

Second, we believe our hunches are wrong, so we ignore the red flags. We think our gut feelings can't be right. So we're engaged in denial and carry on like nothing is wrong because it's easier to deny than to go through the pain of conflict. Your loving partner would surely never do anything to harm or hurt you, right? They promised not to. We disregard our intuition; we ignore the signals, inappropriate conversations, and foggy details. After hearing the explanation from our partner, we assume we must be "crazy," and their explanation is the full truth. It is a dangerous game to question our instincts because it prevents us from understanding the fundamental truths.

Finally, since we have all been inculcated with the belief that marriage and committed relationships are hard work, we disregard red flags. You are meant to fight and negotiate when you're part of a couple, right? Marriage and relationships are hard work, but the battle should not include ignoring your intuition and fighting to be heard, respected, and communicated with as a worthy and lovable partner.

The earlier you start putting your happiness first before you enter into and while you're in a relationship, the better it will be for you. If you value your happiness and peace, you wouldn't want to be with a guy who sends out a lot of mixed messages and red flags. It still boils down to how we allow guys to treat us. You deserve better and you have to stand your ground and expect it because nobody will give it to you.

CHAPTER SUMMARY

- What happens in your relationship depends on what you allow to happen.
- You call the shots in your relationship.
- Study a guy and his behavior to know if he's playing games with you or if he's a keeper.

FINAL WORDS

Ladies have really lost their wonder. We have lost the power we have as the female gender. We have lost who we are supposed to be to societal standards and stereotypes. It's high time we took back our power. It's time to take our lives back from the societal bondage. It's time to flourish and live the lives we've always wanted to live. I hope you find the information in this book helpful.

Manufactured by Amazon.ca
Bolton, ON